"Ame showed me how to change my internal chemistry that stopped my sugar craving permanently. I don't know if I could have ever genuinely changed without her forward thinking advice and delicious desserts! Her nutritious and satisfying recipes along with her gentle guidance are a miracle in my life."

~ Maria Danly, Mill Valley California

"I already considered myself a fairly nurturing person to myself and to those I love, yet after reading Ame's book, I feel inspired to more deeply nourish my creativity both inside and out of the kitchen! This powerful little book will meet you where you are, reawaken your enthusiasm, and help you craft an incredible, delicious life."

~ Susan Moreschi, Sonoma California

Ame is wise, generous and playful! She showed me so many ways to "sweeten" my day to day life and nourish my soul. She has inspired me to awaken all my luscious senses in every moment of living, loving and laughing.

~ Kaer Soutthard, Kentfield California

My mom's desserts are so good, I'd eat her stuff over ANY candy bar any day!

~ Alexander Dunaway, Novato California

My colleagues at work often approach me with an eager gleam in their eyes and ask me, "Do you got any?" The "any" they are referring to are my wife's treats. As you can imagine, my popularity, as well as my energy, has increased significantly since I married her.

~ Philippe Dunaway, Novato California

Sweet Healing

*Free Your Body from Sugar Cravings and
Nourish Yourself with Divine Dessert*

AME WAUTERS

BALBOA.
PRESS

A DIVISION OF HAY HOUSE

Balboa Press books may be ordered through booksellers or by contacting:

Balboa Press
A Division of Hay House
1663 Liberty Drive
Bloomington, IN 47403
www.balboapress.com
1 (877) 407-4847

Because of the dynamic nature of the Internet, any web addresses or links contained in this book may have changed since publication and may no longer be valid. The views expressed in this work are solely those of the author and do not necessarily reflect the views of the publisher, and the publisher hereby disclaims any responsibility for them.

I am not a doctor, nor a nutritionist. I am simply passionate in the arena of health and have been researching and experimenting with food for over 30 years, and I am Certified Holistic Health Coach. I do not make any claims that the recipes or products I offer are a cure for cancer or other diseases.

The information provided in this book is NOT intended as a substitute for the advice provided by your physician or other healthcare professional, or any information contained on or in any product label or packaging.

Do not use the information provided in this book for diagnosing or treating a health problem or disease. Always speak with your physician or other healthcare professional before taking any medication or nutritional, herbal or homeopathic supplement, or using any treatment for a health problem. If you have or suspect that you have a medical problem, contact your health care provider promptly. Do not disregard professional medical advice or delay in seeking professional advice because of something you have read in this book.

Information and statements regarding dietary supplements have not been evaluated by the Food and Drug Administration and are not intended to diagnose, treat, cure, or prevent any disease.

Any people depicted in stock imagery provided by Thinkstock are models, and such images are being used for illustrative purposes only.
Certain stock imagery © Thinkstock.

Printed in the United States of America.

ISBN: 978-1-5043-2631-5 (sc)
ISBN: 978-1-5043-2633-9 (hc)
ISBN: 978-1-5043-2632-2 (e)

Library of Congress Control Number: 2015900325

Balboa Press rev. date: 02/03/2015

To all those seeking the sweetness of life

With Gratitude

For my sister, Camilla, who has been my life-long champion ~ our friendship is a source of deep nourishment.

For my husband, Philippe, my faithful treat-taster and foodie photographer, with whose love and committed partnership, my life is a creative and fulfilling adventure.

For my son, Alex, who inspires me to be my best and reminds me that true and lasting wellness is nourished and sustained with understanding and much laughter.

And to all those sweet-life seekers whom I have had the honor to serve and nurture with my food ~ your vulnerability and desire kindle in me the courage to follow my soul's calling: to feed hope and to offer the delicious wisdom that life is a gift to be enjoyed and relished.

Contents

Something of Me and Why
I Wrote This Book

Several years ago, if you had told me that I could completely heal myself of my sugar cravings, I would have thought, "Who are you kidding? I will *never* be free from sugar's sticky grips. I will *always* have to manage a high level of self-control for the rest of my life!"

I grew up snacking on white bread dipped in white sugar and drinking orange crush soda. (It makes my teeth hurt to think about it now.) By the time I was 15 years old, obsessive thoughts dictated how I spent my day: was I going to bake bread pudding or blueberry scones? I soared on manic highs and plumbed miserable lows, yet still I sought daily pleasure and comfort in sugary things.

While still a teen, I was almost *scared* straight. When I first encountered those early alarming studies – there are volumes of them now – about sugar and the harm it causes, I became confused and terrified. If sugar was so damaging and destructive, why was it an ingredient in so much of our food? I wondered why "grown-ups" weren't doing something about it for goodness sake. In a kind of quiet desperation, I began substituting sugar with what I thought were healthier alternatives, like baking banana bread sweetened with apple juice concentrate. But I could never get these supposedly healthier treats to taste as good as the white sugar versions.

Of course, I had also removed all the fat (as was suggested by the health experts at the time too) but these "better without butter" fat-free cakes were never satisfying – so even while my stomach was full on starch, I still felt hungry. So I ate more! And gained weight.

To my adolescent self, beauty and belonging meant one thing: be thin. So when I gained weight eating mediocre "fat-free sugar-free" food I felt betrayed and deeply resented my body. I began relating to my body like a prisoner of my own private war. If "it" wouldn't cooperate, I would force it to do what I wanted it to do: I would indulge my guilty pleasures then compulsively exercise to work off the self-loathing and guilt as much as the calories.

I could not yet see that I was the one imprisoned, that this way of domination could never happily work out. On this battlefield, I was not able to discern my own body's messages about what I truly needed. And even more demoralizing for me was that I did not know how to respond so I could feel good about myself and have ease and enjoyment around sweets. I couldn't because I had not yet recognized that I was hungering for much more than a sweet dessert.

My battle with sugar cravings and dieting carried on over 20 years. Despite doing my best to learn all the "shoulds & "shouldn'ts," I grew utterly confused and more nervous than nurtured by what I was eating. My struggle with sugar seemed a part of me, like having brown hair and brown eyes; it was genetics that couldn't be helped, not without dreaded sacrifice – like cutting off an arm or shaving my head – something more punishing than the addiction itself.

So if you had told me I could heal myself of sugar cravings, honestly, I wouldn't have dared tell you that I didn't really want to "heal it". I would never embrace a cure worse than the disease and the idea of missing that hit of "happiness," of not having that "little something" to look forward to in my day pained me. I had long figured out that guilt and self-punishment was just the toll I would pay for the short-lived comfort and pleasure. I could tolerate emotional ups and downs, compulsive exercise - and since I had no major illnesses (yet), my sugary diet was do-able.

Sadly, that's what I *used* to think. Before my mother got sick.

I was 36 years old when my still young 77-year-old Mom was diagnosed with terminal cancer. It shook me deeply. I wanted to be there for her – *to feed and nurture her well.* While caring for her - and practically every day since she passed away – I have reflected upon my mother's life: her choices, her wishes, and her wounds. It became crystal clear to me that her health crisis was *my* health crisis. What I wanted for my mother, I want for myself, and also want for you: to love ourselves wholly and not to deny ourselves the sweetness of life. Our cherished desires are not unimportant. Our choices are not inconsequential.

With my mother's passing, beyond the grief came a gift: I could choose to pay a different sort of toll, willingly and consciously. I chose to give up dominating my body and myself, to stop playing self-punishing games of deprivation, over-indulgence, and denial, of doing deals with devils within. ("Devils" are the ones who suggest your choices are of little consequence and that your truest desires do not matter, and worse, are hopeless, selfish and wholly misguided.)

This was a time – and continues to be – of diving deeper – beyond diets and regiments – into the *science of* food. With no small irony, given my mother had colon cancer, my research has taken me into the bowels of our human digestive processes, a literal and metaphoric exploration of *our capacity to be and feel nurtured*, both physically and emotionally.

The more I have learned the more compelling my exploration has become as I continually discover the gifts of healing that our whole foods hold. Let me say simply for now, that two basic things stand out in rare agreement of most modern medical doctors, food scientists and holistic nutritionists: 1) Sugar is highly addictive and is damaging to our body's cells, and 2) plant-based food sustains life. I realize both of these statements might sound profoundly obvious, but when you consider what they mean, they can change the fundamentals of your diet and lifestyle. When I say "damage," I mean *inflammation.* All disease including cancer, irritable bowel syndrome, chronic metabolic disease, arthritis, (the list goes on and on) can be traced to some form of inflammation in the body. It comes down to this basic fact: the less inflammation we have in our bodies, the healthier we stay. Sugar is the most prevalent substance in our diet that feeds and spreads this inflammation throughout our body.

It's important to be aware too that even if you're not eating a lot of desserts, you still may be ingesting a ton of sugar from less obvious sources such as wine and beverages, breads, flours, and other starchy foods, and even fruit. This is why, even before we get to dessert, I will show you how to begin restoring your digestive balance with specific practices and to help you reduce inflammation by introducing food that can heal and feed your immune system.

Having explored the possibilities of plant-based foods, I am thrilled to report that by relying upon these wholesome basics, it IS actually possible to make truly delicious *and* nutritious treats, and I will show you to how to master that alchemical magic. Baking with whole food ingredients and nixing the simple sugar (which also includes white flour), my mind and my mouth have opened wide with the discovery of an abundant variety of nutritionally-sound ingredients with which I can make sweet and satisfying delights. It turns out deprivation was a lie. It was never necessary. Mother Nature has provided everything we need to nourish ourselves well AND satisfy our sweet tooth. We were meant to enjoy ALL the fabulous flavors of our edible world.

I do not have to punish myself *ever*. And neither do you.

This is why I wrote this little book for you. I whole-heartedly believe this discovery process – this opening to an abundant, sweet life-affirming way of being and eating, especially feeling fed and nourished by delicious desserts received from the Divine – is easily accessible, fun, and *fulfilling*.

It will take some sacrifice, though not the kind you may be imagining that involves great suffering. Actually, I invite you to sacrifice your suffering. Is it cynicism? ("Nothing's going to really change for me?") Is it denial? ("Eating sugar not that big of a deal.") Or is it apathy? ("I don't care anymore.") Respect yourself enough to pause here and ask yourself: In what way will I fail to nurture myself? Listen to yourself. You'll hear what is ready to be sacrificed. [In Chapter 2: Step Two: Befriending Your Nurturing Self, we'll address this more fully].

The truth is you *can* nurture yourself. Beyond any sugar-induced highs and lows, beyond the self-punishing trashing and crashing, there is a way to feed your cells well – and have your cake, your chocolate, your pancakes, AND deeply *nourish* and love yourself too!

Let's get underway!

"Wherever you are, whatever you do, be in love." ~ Rumi

A Gentle Journey:
How Best to Use This Guide

You can safely put down your defenses and fears as this is not a book that will further shame you about your desire to gorge on ice cream or reprimand you for listening to that glazed donut that seems to call you by name. Moreover, this means there will be no more guilt-tripping, no more saving up good diet days, so that you can have a bad splurge day. (Yes, let that in). If there's one thing I believe we're *all* learning it is that shaming ourselves does not change anything, but only causes more pain.

Rather, the path unfolding here for you is about learning to listen to yourself with compassion. It's about healing. This means learning to respond with newfound insight and love while becoming more resourceful with the ability to make fantastic new treats that wholly feed and nourish you. It can be a gentle journey, yet profoundly transformative too.

So to be clear, this book will NOT try to inspire you to have more self-control around sugar. There will be no pumping you up and glazing you over with information overload.

Instead, let this small guide be a companion at your side, like a supportive whisper in your ear or a gentle nudge at your back as you too begin to try your hand at new things that will allow you to explore more sweet possibilities. Even if you do not battle constant sugar cravings, you will discover a new way of eating (and drinking too) with deeper satisfaction that will NOT demand sweet deprivation. It's a *personal process* for each of us. What I've tried to do here is map out a way for you to move forward with the least amount of struggle.

While I suspect some of you may want to lunge ahead to the Divine Dessert recipes provided in Chapter 4 – and I celebrate your enthusiasm – since each section has principles and ideas that build on each other, it's important that you harness your eagerness. Focus it upon following the flow of information and guidance as it is presented *step-by-step*. Soon enough you will encounter a divine dessert with your name on it.

Here's why the gradual step-by-step process is important: This book is *not* a diet plan, but rather the opening of a new frontier to explore. While ultimately this will be a place to go wild, creatively engage and discover the sensual enjoyment of whole desserts, **your body will be well served to honor a gentle and gradual approach.**

Each step offered is best experienced consecutively. Until you have done at least some preparatory healing on your body's *chemical* addiction to sugar, you will most likely not be addressing the underlying physical and emotional imbalances that have tripped you up before and may have left you feeling frustrated and defeated. Step-by-step will serve you better.

Once established, these "steps" will work in concert, integrated as routines and practices that will support your daily life with you reaping healthy reward. The recipes included in Chapter 4 will then be a vital resource that will continually serve up divine desserts to a body that's ready to digest and absorb the nurturing pleasure. You will soon be picking and altering the recipes that delight you the most, experimenting with them, and easily making them a part of your daily or weekly routines. (I can see your coconut oil fingerprints staining the pages now!)

As someone who is continually in conversation with her own digestive system, there's one last thing I want to stress: the importance of *going slowly* with dietary change. Our digestion is an extremely complex process and sometimes, especially in the case of severe digestive issues, such as Irritable Bowel Syndrome or Leaky Gut, there will be the necessity to respond to those issues more comprehensively before moving onto the recipe section of this book. In any case, going slowly allows your body, heart, and mind to sync up and work seamlessly together for the long term.

First Things First:
Laying the Foundation for Healing

This guide is practical and action-oriented – I want you in your kitchen stirring up deliciousness – yet I've done my best to include just enough material to guide and inform you so that you are empowered and able to stay the course, and make your way elegantly and creatively forward. For those of you that want to take your knowledge deeper in places, I've included links to resources that I endorse, as they have personally served me well. Otherwise, I will keep you focused only on the essentials that will help you to better understand how to nurture your body and restore and sustain balance and harmony.

I cannot overstate that *this is a journey of healing not merely a recipe book where we substitute sugar* with healthier alternatives. While we're divinely blessed to have healthy sweet options, your ultimate sense of freedom means respecting your physical chemistry and emotional body by learning to deeply attune to your needs.

Let me lay the path out for you. Chapters 1 through 3 provide the information and practices that will provide the foundation for your success.

Chapter 1: Step One ~ Claim Your Chemistry, Honor Your Culture may be the most important step of your journey. The first step often is! Here you'll discover what goes on in your intestinal tract, what generally goes wrong, and how to begin to sort the critical digestive process out so that you are humming along with an enlarged capacity to absorb life-giving nutrients. You'll get to start immediately with a couple of essential new recipes that will alter your interior for the better and continue as a *life-long practice* that will serve to restore and maintain a harmonic bacterial balance. Over time, this "step" alone could free you from your cravings and help to heal chronic digestive conditions. You can think of this as a time when you're preparing the soil for the planting of new sweet seeds of possibility for your life, like enjoying sustained energy or a clearer mind. The more cravings or digestive disorders you tend to suffer, the more gradual your approach should be working with the suggestions of this step. Remember, there is no rush to a finish line ~ the loving preparation of the soil will make for a beautiful garden that you will love attending your whole life long.

At a minimum, you will want to digest its principles and implement its suggestions *for at least 2 weeks.*

Gently we go.

Chapter 2: Step Two ~ Befriending Your Nurturing Self invites you to listen and respond to your complex feeling nature so that you remain in charge of your choices and dreams. Just as we have new food options, here we recognize we have choices beyond self-punishment and denial. Here you are guided through a process to reveal and befriend your "Nurturing Adult Presence" and deepen understanding of what is at the heart of your sweet cravings. Embracing your new nurturing image, you can be inspired to make lasting change in accord with who you are becoming: healthier and more self-loving.

Even while you're in the midst of Step One, you can move onto Step Two. As you expand your capacity to feel and be nurtured, a real and heart-healing sweet life adventure can unfold.

Moving happily along.

Chapter 3: Step Three ～ Feed Your Cells Well is where you'll get better acquainted with what your body actually needs to sustain and regenerate. You'll learn a little about both the **macro**nutrients and all the wonderful **micro**nutrients that are found in whole unprocessed living food. This is the stuff that our physical body is actually craving. Understanding a bit of the basics will also free you up enormously to get creative in the kitchen. Speaking of which…

Now, we are ready for Divine Desserts!

Chapter 4: Step Four ～ Nourishing Yourself With Divine Desserts begins by helping you stock your kitchen with all the cool tools and luscious ingredients you will need to spring into action. Stage set, you'll be served up a variety of sweet recipes suitable for all sorts of everyday celebrations. My hope is that you will soon be getting wonderfully creative adding your own twists and enjoying your truly divine sweet life.

CHAPTER 1

Step One ~ Claim Your Chemistry, Honor Your Culture

Consciously Tending Your Inner Garden

Sugar is faux "sweetness." Over decades now, there has been extensive research done on the chemical addiction that sugary foods cause in our brain. In her book, *The Hunger Fix*, Dr. Pamela Peeke breaks it down plainly: the more sugar we eat, the more we *need* to eat in order to satisfy our body's pleasure centers. In fact, sugar has been shown to be 8 times more addictive than cocaine! With our own brain demanding that we eat more sugar in order to feel "good," we become chemically enslaved with serious disease-causing consequences. Even if you do not have a full-blown sugar "addiction," understand that every time you consume sugar you are dosing your brain with highly potent chemicals that negatively impact its function, which in turn negatively impacts ALL of your organs. Most of us are getting knocked out of whack with some degree of "brain fatigue," moodiness, an inability to stay focused and other unwanted consequences that we end up tolerating as if natural or fated. It is not natural or fated. It is sugar-induced.

The more sugar we eat, the more we feed the unhealthy yeasts and destroy the good bacteria in our gut, which contributes to chronic inflammation in our digestive tract. Hippocrates, who is referred to as the "father of medicine," went as far as to say that all health conditions could be linked back to the digestive process.

Our sugar cravings convince us that we need sugar, when in truth we are hungering for something far more substantive. The craving for sugar simply means we are out of balance. Our purpose here is not to scare you "off sugar" but to offer you something more substantive. We can have our sweet pleasure without ill effect.

Good news: there *is* a simple and accessible antidote to sugar's toxic tyranny.

More good news: It's not a pill or restrictive diet plan. Rather, it involves healing the imbalance that sugar creates in our intestines. *The relief is found in the powerful alchemy of cultured foods.*

Donna Gates, author of *The Body Ecology Diet,* describes our digestive environment as an "inner ecosystem." An ecosystem is a *community of living organisms* interacting with their environment in a powerfully interdependent way and in delicate balance. Having an "inner ecosystem" conjures for me an image of a unique kind of an internal intestinal garden. Cultured food is like the "Miracle Grow" for our gut's garden, supplying our digestive function with the added "good" (probiotic) bacteria it needs to restore and sustain its balance. A thriving inner ecosystem means we have a healthy capacity to absorb nourishment and sustain our vitality.

Basically, cultured foods are probiotic-rich foods made so by adding "friendly" bacteria to vegetables like cabbage, carrots and beets (my particular favorites) and then fermenting for a short time. These bacteria grow and eat the plant matter making the fermented food far more digestible and allowing us to absorb the vitamins and minerals more readily. In fact many vegetables, such as carrots and kale are better not eaten raw, as they are difficult to digest and assimilate. They are far more nutritious fermented or slightly cooked. You can buy cultured foods or even better, you can make them yourself. Making your own not only saves money but also allows you to control the strains of bacteria and yeasts you are consuming. It also ensures that your good bacteria are alive and well. In the pages that follow, I will show you just how easy it is to make your own beautiful batches of cultured veggies.

More and more items are on the market advertising probiotic content. Many of us reach for yogurt thinking we'll get our daily source of probiotics this way. However, some brands of yogurt do not have healthy or even living strands of bacteria in them. (The way a product has been heat processed can kill off the bacteria.) Also, if you can't tolerate dairy, yogurt is not a viable option for you. This is why I emphasize eating cultured vegetables because not only do the vegetables produce virus-fighting bacteria (plantarum) in the fermentation process, but they also will not cause inflammation in your gut due to allergies or food intolerances.

Also, many well-intended folks believe that their probiotic pills are doing the trick. Well, they might be helping your gut to some extent, but pill-form probiotics cannot nearly provide the benefits of cultured vegetables. Two spoonfuls of cultured vegetables are equivalent to an entire bottle of probiotics. In addition, cultured vegetables are rich in vital, absorbable nutrients that are essential to our lasting health.

Unfortunately, it seems many Americans have been scared off of cultured fermented foods because of the fear of bad bacteria making them sick. Just the word "bacteria" can give some folks the "heebie jeebies" even though cultured food practices have been a part of the human diet for thousands of years and are a mainstay of many cultures outside of the US. Sadly, many remain ignorant of the benefits and avoid cultured fermented food.

The fear of cultured foods is misguided. There is a scientific term called "competitive inhibition" which means that *whatever bacterial strains are more abundant win out in a bacterial environment.* Since your gut is a rich bacterial environment, it follows that the more good bacteria we can consume, the more we keep the bad bugs at bay. After all, there are 100 trillion bacteria (more than 10 times our human cells!) in our body. Given that our bodies are made up of more bacteria than human cells, would it not make good sense to feed ourselves these productive "friendly" living organisms? Adding your own potent, friendly bacterial strains ("culture starters") to make your cultured foods means you'll have more "good guys" to eat up the "bad guys."

When you digest these beautiful bacteria, they colonize and form a remarkably collaborative village of consciousness that efficiently clean up the debris in your intestines; they become a strong purposeful force able to fend off various harmful intruders such as viruses, yeast, and other illness-causing agents (agents that LOVE sugar and continually send messages to your brain to consume more of it).

Even more good news: these brilliant bugs also work hand in hand with your *immune system,* which makes sense given that 70% of our immune system is located in our intestines. So, by keeping our gut balanced and cleansed with cultured foods, we not only eliminate sugar cravings, but we are fortifying our bodies' capacity to ward of all sorts of unwanted immune deficiency conditions to which we might otherwise be susceptible.

So think of your gut as *alive*, functioning like a collective brain of microscopic beings that are thriving (or struggling) 24/7. It's an empowering act to hire yourself for the job of repopulating your gut's garden – and give it the "Miracle Grow" of probiotic-rich cultured food on a regular basis in order to keep your garden resilient to pests and actively communicating with your whole body system to keep it thriving.

When we appreciate that there is an important complex ecosystem that thrives (or not) in our gut, and that we can learn to tend to it like we would a beloved garden, cultured foods become an easy addition to our daily routines.

Take note however, if you do suffer from severe chronic digestive issues, such as Leaky Gut (the source of countless digestive issues), you would be well advised to consult with an experienced Leaky Gut Health Practitioner to customize your diet. I would also suggest adding high quality digestive enzymes and Betaine HCL to your diet, while slowly adding in cultured foods, as this illness can be complex to address fully. For more information and help with Leaky Gut, I would recommend visiting http://www.solvingleakygut.com

Now that we know *why* it's important to seed your inner garden, are you ready to discover *how* to tend to your gut's garden?

Eat Cultured Foods and Drinks: Heal Sugar Cravings (and More!)

This essential #1 practice of eating cultured foods will not only curb your physical cravings, but will also awaken your honest emotional desires. (And we believe that's a good thing!) It may take up to 2-3 weeks before you begin to notice your cravings subsiding. The good bacteria need time to eat up all the starving yeast that literally makes our cells scream for sugar. Once you have cleaned up most of that yeast, you can begin to sort out the emotional attachments you have to sweets and channel your energies to truer and more meaningful dreams and desires. (You will learn how to begin to work with this in Chapter 2: Step Two: Befriending Your Nurturing Self.)

We're going to start with something easy, delicious, and effective:

Recipe: Coconut Kefir Water

One of the best ways to ensure a healthy ferment in your cultured food is to use a *culture starter* (which are specific potent strains) to populate the food that you are fermenting. Using a potent culture starter will prevent bad bacteria and unbeneficial yeast from taking over your ferment. You'll be working with a culture starter right away with this foundational recipe.

Coconut Kefir Water is an absolutely wonderful way to get your probiotics everyday. It is not only light and refreshing, but it is immensely cleansing of toxins and heavy metals, while also helping to reduce the production of dangerous yeast (Candida) in your body. By blending in sour fruits, veggies, herbs, and essential oils you will create for yourself super delicious, yet potent tonics. You will be amazed how adding this little drink to your daily routine will dramatically reduce sugar cravings.

Please note: adding living probiotic-rich foods may cause intestinal gas and or diarrhea, which can create some discomfort, so be sure to **go slowly**. No more than 1-2 ounces a day until your body adjusts. Increase gradually to 4-8 ounces a day. It usually takes at least 2-4 weeks for your body to acclimate to its new bacterial residents.

What you'll need:

To purchase Kefir Starter, Culture Starter, and Eco Bloom, you can find the link at http://SweetHealing.com. Look for the Body Ecology link.

Kefir Starter
Culture Starter, optional
Eco Bloom
2 Quart Size Glass Bottles and Lids (available at The Container Store)
4 Cups Organic Coconut Water, Fresh or Pasteurized (available at most grocery stores or Costco)
Heating pad
Small Towels (2)

Once you have your ingredients and supplies ready:

1. Pour 32 ounces of Coconut Water (store bought or fresh from 3-4 young Thai Coconuts) into a 1-quart size bottle. If you are using

fresh Coconut Water, you will want to strain out the pieces of coconut meat.

2. Add ½ packet of Body Ecology's Kefir starter and ½ packet Body Ecology's Culture Starter (I like to use a combination of both for added strains of good bacteria, or you can just use one whole packet of Kefir Starter) to the bottle. The Culture Starter from Body Ecology contains plantarum, an antiviral bacteria, and the Kefir Starter from Body Ecology contains lactobacillus and beneficial yeast.

3. Then, add 1 scoop of Body Ecology's Eco Bloom. This gives the bacteria more food to eat. Especially good to use if you are using a pasteurized, bottled Coconut Water, because much of the sugars have been destroyed in the pasteurization process. The sugars are what the bacteria eat, which in turn, allows them to grow abundantly.

4. Screw lid on tight to keep in the bubbles that will form in the fermentation process. Shake well!

5. Place your glass bottle on a towel-covered heating pad set at LOW, and use another towel to wrap your kefir bottle, as this well help keep it uniformly warm. You do not want to place your kefir bottle directly on the heating pad, as it will get too hot. Be sure to place a towel between the bottom of your bottle and the heating pad. Your Coconut Water should not go above 92 degrees, as the bacteria will not survive extreme heat.

6. Kefir is ready in 36 hours (may vary with varying seasonal temperatures). To check for readiness, move the bottle to one side and see if there are any carbonated bubbles rising to the surface. I make my kefir in the evening or morning so it's easy to remember when to put it in the refrigerator.

7. Once fermented, coconut water will become cloudy and lighter in color. It will have a sparkly, sour, slightly sweet flavor. Your first batch of kefir with the starter packet will be less sparkling than your second. Don't worry about that. **It will be bubblier the next time you make it.** Just be sure to make your next batch within 1-2 days

of completing your last batch. Remember to add more EcoBloom to your next batch.

8. After fermentation is complete, you will want to refrigerate your kefir to extend its life. It should maintain its freshness for about 2-3 weeks, but I always drink my kefir well before then.

Keep It Going: Your Second (and Third, etc) Batch

Pour into your 2nd bottle about ½ Cup of your Coconut Kefir Water to inoculate this batch. Again, be sure to start your new batch within 1 to 2 days of completing your last batch. This will keep your bacteria going strong for months. If you keep your Kefir going within these guidelines, one starter packet can last as long as 2-3 months. Body Ecology's Eco Bloom will also help keep the bacteria alive longer, as it provides food for them to eat. Scoop ¼ tsp. of Eco Bloom in every 1-quart batch you make.

You will know it's time to use a new starter packet when your kefir is less and less sparkling. When this happens do not inoculate your next batch with the last batch. Simply start fresh with your coconut water and starter packets.

How Much To Drink

Remember to go slowly. If you are new to ingesting probiotics, start with 1 ounce per day, and work your way up to 3-4 ounces per day. You can drink it plain or sweetened with a touch of stevia, sour fruit juice, and/or essential oils (more on that later). I like to drink a shot in the morning and in the evening before bed, as it works great to inoculate my system on an empty stomach. It's also helpful to sip some with your meals to help with your digestion. And, if you start to feel a cold or flu coming on it is very helpful to take a shot to help knock it out.

To make your kefir an even more healing, medicinal food, it's time to learn more of the essentials.

The "Magic" of Essential Oils

Once you make your coconut kefir water, you can use it as a base for different tonics and smoothies. An essential ingredient to these delicious potent tonics and smoothies are *essential oils*. These little beauties are far more than nice smelling air fresheners. Therapeutic Grade Essential Oils add potent flavor AND powerful medicine to your diet. They have been used for hundreds of years to ward off infection, increase fertility, kill viruses and bad bacteria, and even cleanse the spirit. In fact, those that survived the black plague used a combination of essential oils to protect themselves. Many of our drugs today are simply synthetic versions of plant extracts. Essential oils work so well because they absorb easily into our cells, healing and rejuvenating us with little to no dangerous side effects.

Just to give you an idea of the potency of essential oils, it takes 28 bushels of lavendar to make just one ounce of lavendar essential oil. The properties of the plant is so concentrated that just 1-2 drops can infuse a quart of water with powerful antioxidents and immune boosting agents.

I use *doTerra Oils* as my preferred brand. I have tried others, but nothing seems to rival the robust flavor of *doTerra*. And, I find the *doTerra* Brand to be of exceptional quality. The main criteria you follow when selecting your essential oils is that your oil be labeled CPTG (Certified Pure Therapeutic Grade) or COTG (Certified Organic Therapeutic Grade).

To learn more about *doTerra* you can visit my site at:
http://SweetHealing.com

Now let's make my favorite daily tonic using your premade Coconut Water Kefir and an essential oil (of your choice). Coming up in Chapter 4, the recipe section, there are additional smoothie recipes that make drinking coconut water kefir a real pleasure.

Recipe: A Cleansing & Alkalizing Daily Tonic

Although, as I've suggested, you can drink your coconut kefir water straight from the bottle, adding a drop or two of essential oil can make incorporating it into your daily diet more pleasing. You can put a drop of essential oil directly in your kefir shot or try the tonic recipe below. This refreshing tonic will not only rehydrate and cleanse your body, but will help significantly reduce any sugar cravings. The ingredients serve to clear out waste in the liver and gall bladder, allowing your digestive system to work more efficiently. The added oils are antibacterial and antiviral, so they also help to boost your immune system. And, the apple cider vinegar helps your body to be more alkaline (less hospitable for inflammation to thrive), while delivering numerous vitamins and minerals.

Make a bottle in the morning, refrigerate, and enjoy it throughout the day. It also makes a great non-alcoholic beverage to serve guests.

Sound good? Let's make it!

Ingredients:

28 ounces of Spring Water
1 tsp. Apple Cider Vinegar
6-8 drops Organic Stevia Liquid
¼ to ½ C. Organic Coconut Kefir Water (see recipe above)
2-3 drops Lime, Lemon, Wild Orange, or Grapefruit Essential Oil (have fun experimenting with different combinations)
Splash of unsweetened cranberry, pomegranate or black current juice

1. Pour all the ingredients in a glass bottle.
2. Gently shake but do not blend in the blender.
3. Store in the refrigerator and enjoy all day long as a refreshing, cool drink to quench your thirst. Makes 4-6 Servings.

If you want your drink to have a slight sparkle, add a splash of sparkling mineral water to each glass you serve.

If you want a deeper cleansing of your liver, include a product called *Livatrex* from Global Healing Center. It is full of medicinal herbs that support and detoxify the liver. Use ¼ bottle of *Livatrex* per quart of tonic mix.

Here are some other creative flavor options for your bottle:

- Add slices of fresh ginger and a few drops of lemon essential oil.
- A lemon-lime fizz by adding sparkling mineral water and a few drops of each oil (to your taste).
- Add fresh sprigs of mint and/or slices of cucumber.

In Summary: Why drink a daily tonic?

- The nutrients and probiotics work together to cleanse the body of toxic buildup, such as heavy metals and unbeneficial yeasts that hinders the good bacteria from flourishing.
- The antimicrobial and antifungal properties of the essential oils coupled with the probiotics help to kill the bad bacteria, such as Candida overgrowth, which is a huge problem in our culture. Candida can be at the root of low energy, difficulty losing weight, foggy brain, depression, sugar cravings, depleted immune function, and over all ill health. It's even now being linked to Alzheimer's.
- The essential oils deliver potent medicinal chemicals that are easy for our body to assimilate, which in turn, allows our bodies to restore and heal more elegantly.
- These drinks will also help to balance your hormones. Yeast overgrowth can create false estrogens, which get stored particularly in our belly fat, so taking probiotics mixed with the oils can help to reduce the weight in that area.

- After a deep cleansing or a liver flush, these drinks will re-inoculate your intestines with the healthy bacteria, and the concentrated plant chemicals will work to revitalize your liver and blood.
- When you are free of toxins and maintain a flourishing internal flora, your body does not crave sugary foods. Thus, you eat and crave more living, nutrient-rich, healing food.
- You will also feel less hungry, especially for sugary foods, so you will likely eat less, allowing weight loss to be easier to maintain.

How to Culture Your Own Veggies

Now that you have mastered your Cultured Coconut Water (Kefir) and are finding how easy it is to incorporate it into your weekly routines, it's time to explore the world of Cultured Vegetables. These require a bit more commitment and perseverance, as it seems more complicated at first. But once you have done it once, you'll see just how easy it is. And, you can make enough to last several months, so it's an effort that really pays off.

Again, you will want to incorporate these potent probioitc foods into your diet slowly as they may produce intestinal gas. Start with 1 Tablespoon 2-4 times a week. Then, over the course of a few weeks, increase to 2 to 4 Tablespoons a day 4-7 times a week. There are lots of ways you can use cultured veggies. I like to mix them in all kinds of salads, or I use the juice to put into salad dressings and soups for added flavor and nutrition.

The recipe below is a basic one that you can feel free to add different spices or other vegetables that you like better.

To purchase the products you need to get started, you can find the link at http://SweetHealing.com. Look for Body Ecology link.

Search for these items:

Culture Starter, from Body Ecology or Caldwell's (another great brand)
Eco Bloom
Ancient Minerals

Donna Schwank, author of *Cultured Food Life*, is an incredible resource for learning more about culturing foods. She can help you to expand your understanding of cultured foods and cultured recipe repertoire. Cultured foods truly are the missing link in our American diet that can take our health to new heights of balance and lasting vitality. Visit her site at: http://www.culturedfoodlife.com. She recommends using Caldwell's Culture Starter, which is also a great starter to make your cultured vegetables.

Recipe: Cultured Ginger Beet, Cabbage and Carrots

This is a fabulous cultured mix that is not only rich in disease-fighting phyto-nutrients, but gives your salads and proteins a gorgeous pop of color and flavor! I like to mix these with lettuce, avocado, chicken salads, eggs, and sausages. It is also fabulous with my Cashew Cream mixed in. See my site, http://SweetHealing.com and search for "Cashew Cream".

6 Medium Carrots, shredded
1 Large Beet or 2 Med. Beets, shredded
1 Small to Med Red Cabbage, sliced thin or shredded
1 Apple, cored
¾ to 1 inch Chunk of Ginger, peeled
2 Med. Garlic Cloves
2 Ancient Mineral Caps from Body Ecology, open capsules
3 tsp. Celtic Sea Salt
1 Packet Culture Starter, (Caldwell's or Body Ecology's)
1 tsp. Eco Bloom from Body Ecology

5 Cups water, add more if needed to cover vegetables in jars
4 Quart Size Jars or 2 half Gallon Jars. (I like to use Bell Canning Jars, the rubber rimmed clamp down jars, or airlock vessels. All of them work well.)
1 Large Cooler (soft fabric version is best) and Heating Pad

How to Make:

1. Add the shredded beets, carrots and sliced cabbage into a very large bowl.
2. Take a handful of these prepared veggies and blend them in your blender along with the opened Ancient Mineral Caps, Eco Bloom, Apple, Salt, Ginger, and Cloves of Garlic with 4 cups of water.
3. Then quickly blend in the packet of Culture Starter. I don't like to over blend my beautiful bacteria.
4. Pour the blended mix over the cabbage, beets and carrots. Add another cup of water to make it a very thick, chunky soup. Mix well. You will need enough water to cover the veggies in each jar, so add more later if you need it.
5. Pack your jars tight and almost full, leaving about 2 inches of room at the top to allow for expansion. Make sure that your veggies are covered in liquid. As the vegetables ferment, some of the liquid may spill out, even though your lid is on tight. That's ok. The gap will help with this expansion. If the water does spill out during the fermentation process, leaving the vegetables uncovered in liquid, open your jar and add more water.
6. Place the jars in cooler (I like to use a soft fabric version, not plastic) with a heating pad underneath the cooler (not inside the cooler). Set heating pad at Medium Heat until the jars are warm to the touch, NOT HOT. It may take an entire day to get there. Then, move the heating pad to low. Keep the jars culturing for 4-6 days (I usually do 4-5 days). Taste your veggies on the 4th day and decide whether you like the taste or would like to culture them longer. The longer they ferment, the more tangy they will become. They

will continue to culture in the refrigerator at a very slow rate. I can keep my veggies for up to 9 months in the refrigerator, as long as they remain unopened.

You may need to add more salt for added flavor after they are fermented. Too much salt can inhibit the growth of the good bacteria, so it is best to add more when they are done culturing. Makes 4 Quarts.

Recipe: Basic Cabbage and Carrot Sauerkraut

1 Napa Cabbage, shredded thin in a food processor
6 Large Carrots, shredded
1 Large Daikon, chopped into small chunks, optional
3 Med. Cloves of Garlic
2 tsp. dried Dill
⅛ to ¼ tsp. Cayenne, optional (gives it a spicy kick!)
2 Ancient Mineral Caps, opened
3 ½ tsp. Celtic Sea Salt
1 tsp. Eco Bloom
1 Packet Culture Starter, (Caldwell's or Body Ecology's)
10-11 Cups of Water
1 Large Cooler and Heating Pad
6-8 Quart Size Jars

How to Make:

1. Add the Cabbage, Carrots, Daikon, and Dill into a bowl.
2. Take a handful of the veggies and blend them in your blender along with the opened Mineral Caps, Eco Bloom, Salt, Cayenne, and Garlic with 4 cups of water.
3. Mix in the packet of Culture Starter. Blend gently.
4. Pour the blended mix over the remaining Cabbage, Carrots, and Daikon.
5. Add more water to make it a very thick soup. Mix well. You will need enough water to cover the veggies in each jar.

6. Pack your jars almost full, leaving about 2 inches at the top to allow for expansion during the fermentation process.

7. Place the jars in a cooler (I like to use a soft fabric version, not plastic) with a heating pad underneath the cooler (not inside the cooler). Set heating pad at medium until the jars are warm to the touch, not HOT. You do not want the temperature to go above 92 degrees, which is comfortably warm to the touch. Once jars are warm, turn the heating pad to low. Keep the jars culturing for 4-6 days. After 4 days taste and decide whether you like the flavor as is or if you would like to culture them longer. The longer they ferment, the more sour they will become. They will continue to culture in the refrigerator at a very slow rate. I can keep my veggies for up to 9 month in the refrigerator, as long as they remain unopened.

Makes 6-8 quart size jars. (If you would like to make more, just increase the amounts of veggies and water. You do not have to increase the amount of Culture Starter.)

You will probably want to add more salt to taste after the veggies have cultured. Adding too much salt while they are culturing can kill the bacteria, so it is best to add more after they are done.

These vegetables make wonderfully flavorful additions to salads, as a side with eggs, stuffed into sandwiches, blended in soups or smoothies, eaten with sausages or burgers, or mixed into grains like quinoa or black rice. The ideas are endless.

Most Important to Remember

Cultured foods cleanse and heal your body. These beautiful foods help to clear the damage and debris that sugar has left behind. More simply put, they are the missing component in our SAD (Standard American Diet). Probiotic pills can help, but eating cultured foods are far more potent and have a whole host of disease fighting, easy to absorb nutrients to boot! Start slowly, but be consistent and you will find a whole new level of immune strength and vibrant health. Be adventurous! Get cultured and you will dramatically increase your nutrient intake while healing your physical sugar cravings easily.

Now, that we have learned about the wonder of cultured foods and their ability to heal the physical cravings for sugar, we can learn more about how to heal the deeper emotional cravings.

"Painful as it may be, a significant emotional event can be the catalyst for choosing a direction that serves us more effectively. Look for the learning." ~ Louisa May Alcott

CHAPTER 2

Step Two ~ Befriending Your Nurturing Self

Healing Old Wounds and Revealing the Heart of What You *Truly* Crave

As children we sought safety in a world that could frighten and overwhelm us. Naturally, we did not yet understand how to create an internal sense of safety or to respond to our own emotional needs so we adapted, using manipulative behaviors to get what we needed emotionally. One of the ways many of us met our needs for love and safety was through eating sugar, candy, and "treats."

In my own childhood, there seemed to be an inherent permission to play and have fun when sugar was present, so it conjures for me a sense of "feeling good." When supplied with sweets (and celebrations or social activities usually involved *some* kind of sugar indulgence), the connection between sugar and warm feelings of safety and being loved were solidified. I equated Sweet Sugar = Feeling Loved and Nurtured. I assert that many of us who habitually reach for sugar (in whatever form) have something akin to this equation going on inside of ourselves.

Synthetic as it may be, and beyond any biochemical imbalance, it's this seductive "delicious feeling" that keeps us *emotionally hooked*, where sugary things are our go-to item for good times and good feelings.

It makes sense why reaching for sugar, including over-indulging alcohol, becomes a way of satisfying a chronic and unmet "need." It is understandable! Meeting ourselves with compassion (not castigation) as we seek to understand ourselves more intimately is so important to our healing journey.

In this Step 2 ~ Befriending Your Nurturing Self, you will get to the heart of what nurturing means to you. We will work with gentle ways to sense your emotional terrain and make the acquaintance of a very real nurturing, loving presence within you that is capable of guiding you – without shame or guilt – in making conscious choices that are right for you. You will learn how to reliably access and befriend and embody this compassionate and wise dimension of yourself that I call your *Nurturing Adult Presence.*

What "Nurturing" is Not: Dismantling the Madness

To begin to better and more reliably attune to this wiser and truly nurturing voice of your *Nurturing Adult Presence,* let's take a moment on the journey to distinguish this voice from a couple of its distorted "faces." In other words, before we listen for what it *is,* let's listen for what it's *not.* You may recognize these two all-too-familiar imposters…

The Indulgent Voice: It is a misguided yet common notion that "a nurturing voice" is a voice that refuses the usefulness of *discipline,* meaning it rejects the need to adhere to supportive structures, nor does it have any need of boundaries. Let's listen to it:

"Yes! Eat and do whatever you want! You *deserve* it! You only live once!" Or, "You've been soooo good all day…you deserve more than a few bites of that ice cream…have the whole pint! Who cares? It's *your* life." Or "Go ahead, eat the whole thing…I know you said you were committed to not eating when you're not hungry, but really what difference does it make? Everybody else does it, why can't I?" Or "If you think it would make you feel better, since you're feeling down and lonely right now, go ahead."

[Pause here for a moment. Listen to your own Indulgent Voice. Does it sound like the above or is it a different twist? Write down what it most commonly says so you can hear it more clearly].

The problem is that this Indulgent Voice has no long-term vision for you. It can't see who YOU are becoming! At least one essential ingredient is missing: your bigger-picture, wiser perspective. With a far too narrow perspective, it provides simple, quick fix "answers" to temporary discomfort that only leaves you hungering for greater substance: real self-love, not some short-sighted mimic. While encouraging your compulsive reactive behaviors, it's actually lying to you by promising comfort and a sense of "nurturing" when it *cannot* deliver it. At our core, we know we want the real deal, so *its quick-fix solutions will never honestly satisfy.*

In a real sense, when we give our power away to this false "nurturing" voice, we are left disempowered, that is to say, we may have *wide permission* but we lack any *real authority* for our lives. This is destructive because it erodes our ability to reliably sense a tether to a fulfilling vision of our future – where a Future Self who embodies our deepest ideals and values lives and thrives. Our compass is thrown wildly off and we cannot discern the difference between self-love and self-delusion.

There's another voice that commonly masquerades as "nurturing" but it too is actually distorting the reading on our Truing-to-Our-Empowered-Future-Self compass.

The Critical Voice: Many of us, having rightly grown suspicious of the Indulgent Voice, lean instead on favoring the Critical Voice. We can hear it as "nurturing" and "positive" because even though it is scolding, derisive, and well, *critical*, we've convinced ourselves it's doing its best to "keep us in line."

For example, the Critical Voice might insist that to be healthier you must have herculean strength and exert high degrees of will power to restrict your cravings. Its façade is much like a drill sergeant, and when you fail to meet its impossible demand of perfection, which you will, you are a loser, weak, and "undisciplined." The Critical Voice then pushes even harder, *whipping you into shape*, and suggesting that you need to abide by even more rules and restrictions. Self-punishment, self-shaming, and deprivation become a viable means to achieve your desired goals.

Let's give a listen: "If you eat that brownie, then you better work out for an hour at the gym…every day this week." Or, "See, I told you you're weak. You blew it. Now you're going to have to starve and eat a very restrictive diet for weeks!" Or, "Okay, you managed to be "good" today, but you better not let down your guard down. You know how you are… you can't be trusted… stay on top of it!"

[Pause here for a moment. Listen to your own Critical Voice. Does it sound like the above or is it a different twist? Write down what it says so you can hear it more clearly].

Trouble is the Critical Voice fails to distinguish *discipline* (which are structures of support and practices designed *by you* to honor what you value and what you want to achieve) and *deprivation*. This voice is *a persistent demand for perfection* that is itself a form of demoralizing and paralyzing self-punishment. Even while "perfection" is an *impossible* demand, the Critical Voice is relentless and will keep convincing you that in order to achieve your health goals, you must seek to attain its unattainable "perfect" image. It will literally harangue you to death trying to achieve it. It is unforgiving – it doesn't even recognize that forgiveness exists - and even if it does, it is not available for *you* because nothing you do is *good enough*. It only sees a need to control your impulses. Like the Indulgent Voice, the Critical Voice does not hold a bigger vision for you. It reminds you of your past mistakes in order to shame and manipulate your decisions and choices. It too does not see your beauty and who you really are.

So, while the Indulgent Voice offers wild and wide permission but urges you to abdicate your own authority to consciously craft your life direction, the Critical Voice stifles any permission and experimentation at all with crushing assumption of its own stern authority to keep you on the straight and narrow. Both are disempowering voices. *Your true empowerment rests with taking your power back and assuming responsibility both for having full permission and full authority of your choices and actions.* No guilt, no shame necessary. Rather you can embrace discipline (i.e. fun structures that support you), compassion, creativity, and forgiveness.

These two dominating voices are unhelpful because they reflect a twisted definition of love and nurturing. Following their prodding and haranguing will not get you the real love and self-caring that you deserve and crave. So, what does it mean to take an honestly nurturing route to health, healing, and living a truly sweet life?

We need to better attune ourselves to the voice of our *Nurturing Adult Presence.*

Letting the Nurturing Voice Be Your Wise Inner Guide

Now that we've looked at what it isn't, what does the Nurturing Voice sound like? Let's begin to map the territory so you can get yourself better oriented and off the mad pendulum swing from Indulgent to Critical and back again. Then, you will be invited to work a powerful process by which you can find and befriend the one you are meant to be: a nurturing friend to yourself.

The "Nurturing Adult Presence" is the voice of your real Future Self who is healthy, emotionally fulfilled, and living a sweeter life than you can yet imagine for yourself. While this "voice" has a bigger vision of possibility for you than you yet have, she will never force you to do anything you do not feel ready or willing to do. She respects you. As your partner, she seeks to understand your present needs and will patiently serve you in finding more honest responses to your internal yearnings. She will give you glimpses of your greatness while helping you to find forgiveness of your shortcomings, and she profoundly believes in your capability.

Your *Nurturing Adult Presence* is your guide to heal old obstructions and refusals and to more fully connect with her as a choice, not a demand. She wisely understands that health is not solely found in a diet and/ or exercise plan and is more a quest for self-understanding. This "you" recognizes that your life is a beautiful gift that you are learning to honor and creatively craft, day-by-day, choice-by-choice. She holds that your purpose is to discover more of who you are, *including becoming someone who can vulnerably receive nurturing from yourself and from your personal world.*

This presence does not judge you but it will tell you the truth. Your *Nurturing Adult Presence* will stir in you a whole new kind of motivation: to love yourself deeply and become more. She remains present with you always, yet honors your choice to attune (or not) to her nurturing and wisdom.

Pause here and REREAD the last two paragraphs. Begin to let your Future Self (Your Nurturing Adult Presence) become a little more real for you. She is with you NOW.

Let's get to know her from the inside.

Outlined below is a powerful process by which you can recalibrate your compass to find and strengthen your partnership with this tremendous capacity to love and nurture yourself. The first step involves assessing where you are now with regard to being self-nurturing. Once you explore and clear away the old "image" of yourself, you will craft a new one more fitting and aligned with the future you who is living her sweet life more fully. Let's not lose another minute feeling lost without a *real* compass!

Process Activity: Embodying a NEW Nurturing Self-Image

We could be offered all the nurturing and love in the world, but if we are not open to receiving it, then nothing changes for us. This is a process that will make much more possible for you.

Note: The most useful and surprising step for me was the first one: free-form writing. I highly encourage you to let your thoughts and feelings flow without concern. Make it safe for yourself to do so…that's being nurturing already! You too may be amazed and surprised by what emerges when you give yourself the permission to write without ANY judgment or critical voice.

Part 1: Revealing (to Yourself) Your Current Self-Image as Self-Nurturing. Grab your journal or some paper because you'll be writing your things down. *Note: Merely thinking about your responses is not the same thing and will not work nearly as well as writing down what you think, feel, and imagine.*

1. **Begin by asking yourself: How am I with nurturing myself?** Write with free association. Don't censor or worry about grammar. You are establishing what you say, do, and think around nurturing yourself. Are you indulgent? Do you give yourself full permission to binge, all the while convincing yourself you are being nurturing? Do you nurture yourself through a high degree of vigilance and restriction? Or condemn yourself if you slip and do something you deem "unhealthy"? Or do you avoid nurturing yourself, except when you are tired or sick? Write until you feel complete. Then stop. Put your work away for at least an hour.
2. Carefully and caringly, read what you've written looking for meaning. Look at any sarcasm, anger, resentment, insight, brilliance, etc. Now, from what you've written, bring it down to a paragraph that captures the *essentials* of your CURRENT self image: "The image I *currently* hold of myself with regard to being Self Nurturing is…."

3. Now bring it down to ONE sentence that expresses the *essence* of the whole paragraph.

4. Now bring it down to a single WORD that encapsulates your image.

5. Good! Now, come up with 5 words that complement that one word, e.g. if your word ended up being "denial" then possible complimentary words for you might be: withdrawn, self-pitying, punishing, lonely, isolated.

6. Whole-heartedly deny this image! Vehemently with feeling! Do this privately and out loud if possible. You may want to take the piece of paper and burn it safely while you state your intention: "I refuse it!" No! No! No! I Release it!"

7. Forgive yourself and others who perhaps encouraged this old image of yourself. Talk to yourself: "When I took that in I didn't know any better. Now I do know better, that's why I'm changing." All those who need to forgive me – I declare it. Forgive others.

Now you have created the space to build a new self-image that will allow you to be more loving and nurturing of yourself and allow more nurturing from others too. Good work! Don't stop here. Let's get building your NEW Self-image! (If you need to take a break before moving on, that's ok, but be sure to get back to it within 24 hours to keep the momentum going.)

Part 2: Building a New Self-Image as Nurturing:
The Secret that Lies in the Heart of Your Nurturing Adult Presence

The heart of your *Nurturing Adult Presence* will embody the very quality you most wanted to experience as a child. It will be the very thing that you most yearned for, and didn't think you could have or didn't know how to create. Instead, you may have used sugar or other adaptive behaviors to simulate this feeling you craved. It may be something that is difficult to articulate because it is so outside your realm of experience to date, yet this feeling is also in some way the most obvious because it is what you are *seeking all the time*. In this phase, you may find yourself thinking back to when you were a child. What did you yearn for then? Allow yourself to write freely. This exercise will loosen your mind and connect you to your heart. In so doing, the process will allow your heart to speak openly. As you read between the lines, the core of what you truly crave will emerge from your consciousness, much like a gem emerges from carefully cut stone.

1. Write down the words "Nurtured" or "Nurturing." Touching in with your heart and soul, what other words support what *you* mean when you conjure the feeling of being nurtured and nurturing? (e.g., generous, kind, understanding, empathetic, loving, etc.)
2. Now choose *one* of those selected words. Which word pops out and speaks to your heart?
3. Expand that one word into a sentence describing what it means to you as someone who embodies this quality.
4. Build that one sentence into a paragraph further exploring what it means to you.
5. Then, expansively free-write. Get into it: What is this nurtured and nurturing person like embodying more of this quality? Explore who you are and becoming even more of.
6. Now imagine yourself BEING this one wholly, and feel the new image as yourself. Perhaps you close your eyes and sense it more intensely or you stand up and adopt the posture of this one. Step into being this Nurturing Adult Presence. What changes in your experience? What's different about this "place"?
7. Affirm. Embrace. Accept. Say, out loud, and from a mountaintop (meditatively or take a walk up a hillside!): "I am a Nurturing Adult Presence and I am becoming [fill this in]! "I own it, it's mine." Declare it! Befriend her. Lean on her. Engage in conversation with her. Remember her. Every day.

A simple, powerful way to remember her: CELEBRATE! Draw a heart and write your word(s) inside of it. Let it be a symbol of what is at the heart of your *Nurturing Adult Presence*. Post your heart and word(s) where you will see it everyday. Let it become a part of your new nurturing image.

Great work! Expanding your self-image is powerful work that never stops. You can return to this process whenever you are inwardly called to upgrade your self-image so that you might allow more love, nurturing, and success into your life.

Below, I share a bit about my own process building a more nurturing self-image. If you have not yet done the process (as described above), I hope that you will read my words and be encouraged to go for it. It's important because *you are important.*

By Way of Encouragement: My Personal Process

As I let myself freely write about my old image of how I nurtured myself, I noticed a constricting feeling lurking in the shadows of my consciousness, yet I couldn't quite articulate what it was about. I continued to write freely. Then, I became aware of certain conditions and "rules" to which I had unconsciously been abiding. I realized that I had to have a "justifiable" reason to nurture myself. It wasn't "okay" to nurture myself just for the sheer fun and enjoyment of it. It felt too indulgent to nurture myself for no reason.

When I distilled the old image paragraph to just a few words, I was even more curious to notice that some of the words that popped out were "reluctant" and "threatened." I finally landed on the word "scared." I felt *scared* to nurture myself fully. I sensed the "young me" inside was convinced she would get in trouble if she generously gave love and nurturing to herself. She felt she would be betraying an old agreement that she had made a long time ago with her mother. My mother did not nurture herself and out of my desire to feel connected to her, I had made an unspoken agreement not to nurture myself either. As I sat with these feelings that had been buried for years, I reread my writing. I understood that the immature part of me had made this pact with her mother out of love and a need to survive, yet I also saw that it was no longer serving me or anyone else. After feeling the pain of the past, it was easy to forgive myself and forgive my mother.

I then made a new declaration that I would give myself permission to enjoy my life fully, no longer letting myself be controlled by a looming and ambiguous sense of guilt for living a fulfilling and nurturing life. As I burned my old image, I watched the smoke drift up into the chimney. As it turned to ash, I felt an easy, gentle release in my chest.

In part 2 – Building a NEW image, the word that conjured a feeling of love and nurturing with all its bounty for ME, was "playfulness." Again, I felt surprised. The word "playfulness" from my adult's perspective felt full of creativity and pleasure. With this new word, my world is tinted, not tainted, with more vibrancy and possibility. *I saw that this quality of playfulness was at the very heart of what I had most yearned for as a child.* It was what I had most *craved* yet couldn't get to my satisfaction.

Now, with this new understanding, I can consciously bring the qualities of "playfulness" into my life. The way I greet my day in the morning can have a sense of anticipation for what fun awaits. I don't have to motivate myself out of a sense of fear or obligation. Rather, I can be compelled by a sense of creative exploration to learn and achieve new things. My way of "being" with myself, and others is now more naturally kind, generous, and light-hearted.

Making this real in my day is a new kind of *discipline* that my whole body, heart, and mind embraces. This new way of being has become a part of *me*.

Nurturing Disciplines: Designing Practical Enjoyable Ways to Care About Yourself Daily

You've made a commitment to your Future Self who knows how to love herself "good enough" and who is lovingly living her sweet life.

She whispers to you the nurturing way to becoming her. Why not design some daily or weekly practices that honor that commitment? Here are some suggestions that I hope you'll pick from and/or add to the list:

- ~ Place the heart you have drawn with your word(s) inside of it all over the places in your life. Put one on your desk, your bathroom mirror, or your car. Let it hold the resonance of nurturing for you as you go about your day.
- ~ Throughout the day, rather than judge yourself, instead make it a practice to "bear witness" to the thoughts and feelings inside you, listening with love and without trying to change them or get rid of them. Then make your choices by consulting with your *Nurturing Adult Presence*. What does she say about how to respond to your emotional needs? Stay in conversation with her.
- ~ With the word you have chosen, the one that speaks to the heart of your *Nurturing Adult Presence*, do something consciously that will express that quality or experience. Consciously conjure this new image whenever and wherever possible, even if it is just for a moment. For example, my word, "playfulness," embodied the essence of my *Nurturing Adult Presence*, so as I wake up each morning I make a point of being playful with my dog, or joking around with my husband to consciously bring in that "sense of play" to start my day. This nurturing energy then carries over into all the various aspects of my day, such as, what choices I make around my diet and exercise, work and relationships. Let yourself witness a new kind of motivation emerge, one that is aligned with your new, more nurturing image.
- ~ If you like to journal, engage in conversation with your *Nurturing Adult Presence* and ask her to help you. Write about where you keep getting tripped up and need more guidance. It is a powerful practice to talk to that *Nurturing Adult Presence* through pen and paper. You will be amazed at the wisdom that spills out when you look through her lens and dialogue with her.

~ Using a buddy to share your insights and commitments is also a powerful way to stay engaged and inspired with your new future self. Pick someone you trust and go through the process together.

What nurturing disciplines call to you? To what will you commit? Write it down where you can read it everyday.

What's Most Important to Remember

Remember to give whatever you learned from the above process *realness*. Let it change the way you see yourself and the way you see your life. We cannot sustain change, no matter how much we try, if we do not heal the source of our negative emotional patterns. The process above is designed to help you get at the root of those negative patterns and it allows you to access what has heart and meaning to YOU. Once you know what that is, it is easy to remind yourself of who you are becoming. Make a commitment to at least one nurturing practice. Then, let new choices about how you eat and live flow from the brilliant future you envision. Let the old motivations fueled by harsh demands or careless abandon shift into an inspired desire to heal and feel more alive. Allow more self-love to permeate and transform your thoughts, your feelings, and your life.

If you have any comments or questions or just want to share with me you personal process, send me a message at: http://SweetHealing.com

You've done good work: you have discovered cultured foods, cleansed, and become acquainted with the heart of your nurturing self. Now let's learn more about how to nourish your cells.

*"Let food be thy medicine, and medicine
be thy food." ~ Hippocrates*

CHAPTER 3

Step Three ~ Feed Your Cells Well

Know Your Sugars and Get More
Aquainted with Your Nutrients

Let's Start with Sugars and Sweetners

Unfortunatley there are NOT a lot of products out on the market
that use the healthier sweetners and sugars, or if they do, they use too
much which woefully renders the food almost inedible. Perhaps as
consumer demand grows we will see more companies creating truly
healthy products but *you* do not have to wait.

Which Sweetners to Use and Which Ones to Avoid

There is a lot of information out there about what sugar substitutes are
okay to consume and which ones are not. You can get whiplash trying
to stay abreast of the latest research. I've assembled below a simple list
of the sweeteners that I like and am comfortable using, and those that
I generally avoid.

Use these lists for guidance as you navigate your dietary world.

Sweeteners I Like and Recommend:

1. Stevia Powder and Liquid. Be aware that not all stevia is the same. It varies greatly in its potency and quality. KAL and Omica are the brands I use most often in my recipes.
2. Monk Fruit Extract, similar to Stevia. Very sweet, use in small amounts.
3. Xylitol can work great for some. Just be sure to buy from a reputible source that does not use harsh chemicals for processing. And, be sure not to eat too much at one time, as it can have a laxitive effect. It's sweetness is equal to cane sugar, so keep it to 1-2 tsp's a day and see how it works for you.

2 Servings of Any Combination Per Day (aprox 10 grams of sugar per day):

1. Raw Honey, no more than 1 tsp. per serving
2. Maple Syrup, no more than 1 tsp. per serving
3. Medjool Dates, no more than 1 per serving
4. Coconut Palm Sugar, no more than 1 tsp. per serving
5. Yacan Syrup, no more than 2 tsp. per serving

NOTE: All sweeteners are NOT created equal. For instance, the Stevia I buy from Trader Joe's is far less sweet than the KAL Brand I recommend. 3 tsp. of the Trader Joes Brand was equal in sweetness to ⅛ of a tsp. of the KAL Brand of Stevia. That's a huge difference!

So, in the recipe section of this book, please be aware that if you use other brands than are suggested, you may need to modify the amounts indicated.

Sweeteners I Avoid:

Evaporated Cane Juice (basically the same as simple sugar)
Agave (too high in fructose)
Splenda and Equal (brain altering chemicals)
Aspartame (brain altering chemicals)

A Note About Soda

Soda, both regular and diet, continues to be a large source of sugar and/or chemicals in our diet. Both increase cravings for sugar. So, as an extra little gift I want to offer you a wonderfull refreshing alternative that doesn't do damage to your beautiful brain and bones. And it will save you money too.

Receipe: Ame's Soda Alternative

Buy a quality sparkling mineral water (be sure it is naturally sourced meaning it *actually has minerals* in it) and add a drop or two of peppermint, lime, lemon, or grapefruit essential oil. Whatever flavor is to your liking. Then add a few drops of stevia to sweeten it to your personal taste. (Of course, adding a bit of Coconut Kefir makes it even better!) I think you will be amazed at the refreshing flavor. And best of all, you will be bolstering your bones and brain, not undermining their function. You can keep the oils and liquid stevia in your car, so you can even make your drinks on the go! Easy peasy.

Nourish Your Body with Macro and Micro Nutrients

What are macro and micronutrients? If you want your body to be optimally nourished, you want to know! Macro Nutrients are Proteins, Fats and Carbohydrates. Micro Nutrients are just as essential to good health, but we need them in smaller amounts, thus they are the micro part of the equation: the vitamins and minerals we need to keep our bodies humming along happily.

The world of macro nutrition is vast and varied and what may be a good source for one person may be a disaster for another; so, I cannot begin to tell you which ones to eat and which ones to avoid…at least not entirely. As I've said, this book is not a diet plan but rather intends to serve as a guide to help you on your journey to greater vitality while enjoying yourself. Discovering what works best for you will be part of your personal discovery. However, I CAN distinguish for you the nutritional basics and perhaps debunk some old myths and ideas. You CAN avoid known pitfalls and journey with greater elegance and ease.

Know Your Key Nutrients: Healthy Fats and Protein

We often crave sweets when we haven't gotten enough Macro Nutrients, **particularly healthy fat and protein**. (Carbohydrates are the more complex piece of the equation. I'll save that for a bit later.)

Let's start with the fats, especially since some of us still think fat makes us fat. That's our first big fat myth to bust! Our brain is made of fat and it's absolutely imperative that we eat it regularly to keep it fortified and fabulous. Also, an important fact to digest: we need fat in order to absorb all the colorful, health providing pigments in our veggies and fruits. Without fortifying fat, all that goodness cannot be absorbed into our bodies.

Here's the Skinny on Fats that I Suggest:

Avocados (great to eat with animal proteins)
Avocado Oil (ok to cook with)
Organic Extra Virgin Cold Pressed Coconut Oil (ok to cook with)
Cacao Butter (melted down for chocolates)
Red Palm Oil (ok to cook with)
Raw Nuts and Seeds, all kinds (except peanuts)
Extra Virgin Organic Olive Oil (not good for cooking at high temps, better to drizzle after cooking)
Grass-Fed Butter (if dairy tolerant. Easily burns, add in at the end of cooking)
Grass-Fed Ghee (ok to cook at higher temps)
Grapeseed Oil (ok to cook with)

A Bite More About Nuts and Seeds

Roasting nuts and seeds destroys their health properties, so it's very important that when you buy your nut butters and oils that they are NOT made with the roasted variety. Also, most nuts and some seeds have what is called an enzyme inhibitor. This enzyme makes it very difficult to digest your nut or seed, so it is important to soak and rinse your nuts and some of your seeds before you eat them. This process releases the enzyme, and makes the nuts or seed 6 times more digestible.

When you buy your nuts, simply pour a few cups of almonds, sunflower seeds, or walnuts in a container, cover them with water overnight, then rinse and dehydrate the next day. After dehydrating, store them in your pantry in an airtight container, and use them as needed. I will discuss more about how to do this in the pantry section ahead.

If you want to use the soaked nuts or seeds in a blended drink or salad dressing, there is no need to dehydrate. Just rinse, blend, and enjoy in your dressing or smoothie. Remember to be sure to eat them within a few days, as they will go bad easily after they are soaked.

If you find that you are gaining weight with eating more fats, check out the source as you might have a food intolerance or digestive issue. For instance, not everyone can tolerate dairy, so butter might not work well, but Ghee will work wonderfully. Too many nuts and seeds are also often a weight gain culprit.

So again, go gently with dietary changes. If you your body is used to a low fat diet, add fats in slowly and pay attention to how your body feels and reacts before making any needed adjustments.

Now let's explore *proteins*.

Which Proteins are Best?

Whether you rely on protein found in plant-based foods or animal sources, your choices of protein will naturally be part of your personal discovery process. Personally, I eat both. My only criteria in selecting ANY protein are that it be of high quality. For instance, grass-fed beef is not the same food as beef that has been raised on corn. Cows are not meant to digest corn. It makes them sick and fat, which in turn, does the same thing to us. I know it costs a bit more to buy from organic local farms, but choosing these foods when you can, will make a huge difference to your health and enjoyment.

If you've never had eggs from chickens that have been able to run around the yard eating grubs and bugs, then you haven't yet experienced the delicate, luxurious, beauty of an egg. Most people do not realize that chickens are carnivores and do not thrive on GMO'd corn either! Organic or not, corn is not the greatest food for birds. They like bug protein. The most nutritious part of the egg is the yolk. The choline in that sunny center is fantastic food for our brain. When the chickens eat all the protein rich bugs, the yolks are exponentially filled with anti-inflammatory Omega 3 Oils. In fact, the white part can be discarded altogether. Not that I suggest you do that, but if you have digestive issues, you may want to try it. Raw egg whites should be avoided altogether, as they contain a harmful toxin. So, if you want that extra protein in your smoothie just use the raw yolks, not the whites. You can't go wrong with a poached or soft-boiled version. They are wonderful with a little dollop of cultured vegetables and avocado. Also, a great tip to remember: eat avocado with your animal protein. Studies have shown avocado helps to reduce possible inflammatory responses when consuming animal protein.

Proteins found in the plant kingdom are wonderful and varied. Chia and Hemp seeds are some of my potent favorites. They add wonderful texture and crunch to smoothies and are filled with Omega 3 Oils, minerals, and vitamins. These do not require soaking before consuming.

Again, your protein needs are very individual. It will be up to you to experiment and see which ones work best to sustain your energy and appetite. Protein is essential in helping ease your cravings for ANY kind of food, not just sugar. We need our protein to rebuild our bones and tissues, as our body is constantly regenerating itself, so choose wisely with this important building block.

The one rule to pay attention to, at least most of the time, is eat your proteins with vegetables and fats, not starchy stuff. Keep the starchy food separate. And, include cultured vegetables. Not only will your dishes taste better, but it will also be less taxing to digest. Remember, the easier we make it to digest our food, the better our immune system will fight against disease. For added digestive support, I would also suggest taking a high quality enzyme with your meals, especially if you are having both a starch and protein together. If you are over 50 and still have digestive issues, even after taking enzymes, try including Betaine HCL to help increase the stomach acids in your stomach.

I remember when I was concerned about losing weight I used to avoid proteins and fats, thinking that they would make me fat. I bought the party line about fats causing weight gain and protein being too hard to digest so I would choose a whole grain salad, oatmeal bar, or rice dish instead. Trouble was, not only were those options harder to digest, I didn't feel satiated for more than 2 hours, so I'd end up craving my sugary treats 2-3 hours later, plus I gained weight and felt more tired.

Now, I like to couple my proteins with some healthy fat, like avocados, non-starchy veggies, and cultured foods, and my digestion is far more efficient. I also feel more nourished. I'm no longer hungry all of the time. Best of all, my energy stays steady throughout the day, I don't feel bloated, I maintain my weight, and I no longer struggle with ANY cravings.

Here's a list of Proteins I Suggest:

Grass-Fed Meats
Farm Raised Chicken and Eggs
Wild Caught Fish (no Shellfish, as it's just too toxic)
All kinds of Seeds (Hemp, Flax, Chia, Sesame, Pumpkin, Sunflower Seeds) Rice Protein (in moderation, as rice does contain metals)
Grass-Fed Whey
Organic Dairy, fermented, raw, or low temp pasteurized is best (if you can tolerate dairy)
Small Beans, in moderation. Adzuki's are great.
Algae's, Chlorella, and Spirulina

Must I Curb the Carbs?

There seems to be a lot controversy about what carbohydrates to eat. Vegetables, especially the colorful kind, are not so much in question. Fruit is good too as long as it's eaten in moderation, due to the high sugar content found in most varieties. Berries make a great choice because of their lower sugar content.

It's the starchy grains and starchy veggies that have most of us confused. We all know that colorful vegetables and fruit provide a wonderful array of disease fighting phyto-nutrients, anti-oxidants, enzymes, and fiber, yet aren't grains rich in these elements too?

This is a great question, and once again it is an individual choice and has to do with your ability to digest and absorb the food you are eating. Most folks I talk to, especially those over 40, do better without gluten or a lot of grains. Naturally, it is up to you to decide whether or not grains work for your digestive system, yet understand that every grain is different. So experiment and see what makes a difference to your system. Do be aware that rice has trace levels of arsenic and cadmium in it, even the organic kind, so it's best to eat it in moderation. (This includes Rice Protein Powders). Gluten has also been shown to gunk up the intestines and lots of folks have difficulty digesting it.

My favorite grains are really more like seeds. They do not have gluten, and they are rich in proteins, vitamins, and minerals. They are Quinoa and Millet. Quinoa is rich in protein and Millet is one grain that is actually alkaline forming in the body. I still do not eat grains in large quantities everyday, but a little here and there helps me get more variety in my diet. These grains also help to produce serotonin in the brain, the happy hormone that helps us sleep better at night. So choosing to eat your grains for dinner is a better option than eating them for lunch, as they will help you relax and fall sleep more easily. But again, the most important guideline to follow when eating grains and protein is that you include cultured food to your meal. Whether it be eating cultured vegetables or sipping on some coconut kefir water, you will fare better in the digestive department.

If weight is an ongoing issue you for you, I would look to eliminating grains or at least experiment with different kinds of grains to see which ones work and which ones need to be eliminated.

Get Super and Spicy!

I had to include at least a note about spices and super foods, as they are such an important part of our diet! They not only make our dishes light up with flavor, but they bring powerful healing agents to our bodies.

The most important anti-inflammatory spices to eat regularly:

Ginger
Turmeric
Garlic
Cinnamon

I've also found including fresh parsley, fresh cilantro, fresh basil, fresh mint, oregano, fennel, sage, and lavender make up an essential mix of nutrient-rich flavors. These miraculous plants are the "touch of magic" that not only allow us to enjoy our food and make our meals pop with gorgeous color, but they help us guard against disease. Parsley for instance, is full of calcium, so you can ditch the dairy and load up on these tasty greens, and Cilantro is a powerful cleanser of heavy metals.

In the recipe section you will also find various super foods included in the pantry list. These foods are called "super" for a reason. They are super dense in disease fighting, immune boosting agents that enrich your diet exponentially. It would be a super shame not to include them!

Use Spices and Super Foods! They will help keep you and your life super healthy.

Easy Dietary Guidelines to Remember:

1. Eat high quality protein and healthy fats at every meal, and you won't make your body scream for quick calories. The proteins and fats in our diet cut the sugar cravings because they are dense in nutrition and slow to absorb. It's much harder to lust after a Cinnabun if your body is full on these more dense and complete foods. And, a great little tip: eat avocado with your protein. Avocado helps to reduce possible inflammatory responses when consuming animal protein.

2. Swap the starchy carbohydrates for non-starchy veggies, at least most of the time. Enjoy the fresh, colorful veggies of each season (with a little fat too, of course).

3. Eat protein with fats and non-starchy vegetables, not grains. When you do eat starchy carbs do not eat them with protein, at least most of the time. It is far easier on your digestion to eat starches and proteins separately.

4. Add some cultured veggies or sip on some cultured kefir water with your meals to bring in the probiotic punch. The bacteria transforms

the vitamins and minerals into easily absorbed nutrition, helps you cleanse and digest your food, and adds incredible virus fighting agents to your diet.

5. Spice it up! Refer to the spices I listed earlier. Garlic is a must. And, keep a fresh bunch of parsley, cilantro or basil on hand. It will not only make your dishes beautiful, but will add delicious, healing nutrition. Super foods are also an incredibly effective way to exponentially increase your nutrient intake. (In the next section I'll introduce you to some of my favorites.)

Now, let's learn more about this "New Frontier of Food".

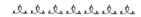

"The world is but a canvas to the imagination."
~ Henry David Thoreau

CHAPTER 4

Step Four ~ Create Nourishing Divine Desserts

Where the FUN really begins: Make Your Own Treats!

Ever since I was just a little girl, I've loved cooking and baking in the kitchen. I am the last of six kids, so there was always a very willing army of eager mouths delighted to eat whatever I made. I loved the entire process of cooking: measuring, mixing, and dreaming up new and creative concoctions with my ingredients. I felt like a magician whipping up happiness and joy. I especially loved making sweet treats because they got my family and friends the most excited.

In all their shapes, colors and textures, desserts have always allowed me to tap into that sense of gratitude and joy for being alive.

Always at the heart of every celebration, this sort of deliciousness never ceases to make the people around me relax and smile. It is generosity, play, and fun all wrapped into one.

In the pages that follow, I have put together a sampling of some of my favorite dessert recipes that will not only satisfy your "sweet treat" moment, but unlike the simple sugary kind, these Divine Desserts will also nourish your body into greater health and well-being.

As you mix up the nourishing magic, also be aware of what thoughts and intentions you'd like to stir in. Perhaps add some happiness with a sprinkle of love, or a pinch of compassion and a drop of joy. Have some fun adding in *your* unique emotional ingredients, and take note of how these feelings begin to blossom more abundantly in your life.

I do have one cautionary flag on the field: these are so good that if your indulgent voice has you in its grips, you may be tempted to binge. Remember that these "desserts" are real food not fluff. We have not merely substituted simple sugars with sweeteners of a different kind. We have made an effort to bring out the natural sweet flavors of the ingredients. Savor and enjoy these Divine Desserts.

Having sincerely implemented the suggestions in Chapters 1-3, you will likely find that you do not have the urge to overeat. In fact, one of the telltale signs that your body is healing is that you will NOT be as hungry for sweet treats (or overeating anything for that matter!) As our bodies become more nourished, both physically and emotionally, with quality food and quality experiences, we won't feel the compulsion to reach for something to fill that "empty" space because we will be full on the honest *goodness* that we have allowed in our lives.

So be sure to pay attention to your cravings and listen to them carefully. If you are finding yourself eating more than just a few treats a day, you may want to go back and reread Chapters 1-3 and go deeper with your personal "nurturing" process.

Also, please note that if you are someone who has severe Candida, Leaky Gut, or any other chronic intestinal issue, recipes with nut butters and coconut flours are not the best to start with. Any flours, including gluten-free flours, can exacerbate intestinal infections. It is best to steer clear of ALL flours and reduce your nut butter intake until your body can find balance again. I say this not to discourage you but rather to encourage you to stay on your path of digestive healing. Once you have cleared up those issues, your diet will allow for more options. There is indeed a light at the end of your tunnel and it is a tasty one!

Before we move to the recipes, I want to first introduce you to some of the building blocks, new tools and ingredients that you may not be familiar with and accustomed to using. Then, you'll be all set up and ready to dive in!

The Raw Facts

In order for us to make our super healthy snacks and treats we need to learn about the wonder of using raw food. The raw food I am referring to includes vegetables, fruits, nuts, seeds, spices, and herbs. Eaten in their raw form, these foods have their natural enzymes and micronutrients intact, allowing our bodies to assimilate the nutrition more easily, and thus giving us more energy and health protecting chemicals.

The fats found in plants are also wonderful for your body. You will eat less volume with raw food because the healthy oils found in coconuts, ghee, nuts, and seeds will help you feel more satiated. And, since the sugars are not processed and are absorbed more slowly, your energy will be sustained for longer periods of time. You will end up eating less because your body is being fed more nutrients. It's not the calories that feed us, but rather the absorbable nutrition that nourishes our bodies. When we eat processed food, our cells literally hunger for the missing components.

When we enter into the world of dehydrating nuts, seeds, fruits, vegetables and spices, we are ushered into a new frontier of crunchy, easy to store, easy to transport, nutritious snacks.

Raw food is also more easily released from our bodies, unlike gluten and other flour products that tend to clog up our delicate systems.

As for the medicinal properties found in plant-based foods? Well, it's endless. Food is medicine, yet it does not have to TASTE like it! When we eat food that heals AND tastes delicious we are rejuvenated and we feel more ALIVE.

Obviously, being healthy requires a lot more than a diet rich in raw foods, but what we eat plays an integral part. Exercise, developing and expressing our passions, loving our friends and ourselves, feeling connected, and expressing how we feel, are all part of the longer longevity recipe. I have found that eating more living food (food that still has enzymes, healthful fats, and super nutrients in tact), allows us to bring these important parts of our lives into greater focus and clarity.

Are you ready to have a vibrant, disease-free body well into your mature years, enjoy your life, and not feel deprived of good tasting, healing, fast food? Great! You will need a dehydrator, high-speed blender, and a food processor.

In the pages that follow I will explain each tool and offer simple recipes to get started. Believe me, all of it is easy to learn.

Now, let's get to the kitchen!

Prepare Your Kitchen For Sweet Success

The following items are ones that I use all the time when preparing my desserts. These are the first things I recommend you buy in your endeavor to learn more delicious and nutritious recipes.

High Speed Blender

There are really only 2 options on the market today that I recommend. The Vitamix and The Blendtec. Both are wonderful, however the Blendtec is easier to clean. The reason these blenders are so essential is because they are able to liquefy your ingredients to such an extent that you can make creamy sauces, sorbets, and smoothies like never before. I know it is an expensive piece of equipment, but you have to see it as an investment to your health. When you have the tools, you make the changes. Don't skimp on your life. Believe me, it's a tool you will use multiple times a day and you will soon wonder how you lived without it. To learn more visit my site: http://SweetHealing.com

Food Processor

Many of my recipes use the food processor to mix up raw cookie dough or shred vegetables for culturing. Mine is small enough to live on my counter, which I like. However, it can be challenging for larger projects, but since I do those rarely, I like the small version for convenience' sake. Again, this is an essential tool for your creative, healthy kitchen. You will use it for desserts and making your cultured vegetables. You will need a blade for shredding, and one for slicing thin slices in addition to the internal blade it comes with.

The Dehydrator

This is one tool that I've noticed folks have the most resistance to purchasing. I think they have images of it becoming a large black box gathering dust in the corner, and the idea of learning how to use it just feels too intimidating. Well, I'm here to tell you that a toaster oven looks like rocket science next to this essential, easy-to-use appliance. You will be marveling for years to come over its wide range of delicious goodies that pour forth from its sliding door. You simply spread your food onto the Paraflex sheets (you need to buy these separately) that lie on your plastic trays, slide your tray into the box, set your temperature, and let it dry.

I've done some research for you, so if want to consider purchasing a dehydrator begin by checking out my recommendations on http://SweetHealing.com (I do receive affiliate fees – yet regardless, I only recommend my tried and true favorites!)

I think you'll be pleasantly surprised with how versatile and easy-to-use a dehydrator can be: it allows you to make a wider range of edibles with lots of different textures, such as crunchy snacks, cookies, and fruit chewies while also maintaining the wholesome goodness of your ingredients. If you're on the Paleo Diet, you can really start to crave that crunch, since grains are no longer an option. Using nuts, seeds and vegetables to make your crackers, cookies and cereals is a revolutionary way to still get that crunch AND maintain your dietary needs.

When traveling, where it is often difficult to get a nutritious bite on the go, I always have a little airtight box of crackers or cookies in my purse and I'm able to sustain my energy. I also don't have to waste time and money searching for something to eat while away from my plentiful pantry.

Containers

It's very important to have lots of containers for all the wonderful things you will be making, and stuff you will be soaking. They must be airtight to allow your treats to last for many weeks. I like the BPA-Free ones at Costco, or you can find all kinds of shapes and sizes to suit your kitchen at The Container Store. Just make sure your containers are Glass or BPA-Free Plastic.

Miscellaneous Supplies

You will also need a glass 8 x 8 Pyrex pan, wooden spoons to spread our mixes, a muffin tin, paper muffin cups, and parchment paper to line your pans.

A New Frontier: New Ingredients, New Techniques, New Food

As I mentioned before, this little book is an entryway into a new Frontier of Food. I call it the "New Frontier" because much of it is fairly undiscovered territory and it will bring you back in touch with the natural beauty and pleasure of whole food.

Below are a few must have ingredients that I keep in my pantry all the time so that I can whip up easy, healthy snacks in a jif. Please note that many of the following ingredients come from various places all over the world, and will vary in taste and quality. I would suggest buying organic as much as possible, as the flavor and health benefits are superior.

The recipes I have included are specifically designed to be rich in healthy fats, proteins, and some natural sugars to help you feed your body what it really wants: real whole food. Since they are so dense in nutrients, you should not feel the need to overeat them. Instead, let yourself savor the textured sweetness. I have given you just a sampling of what is possible, so as not to overwhelm you, and to give you a taste of new ingredients and tools. This book is just the beginning of your adventure into the new Frontier of Food and is designed to help you build a strong foundation which to explore and discover ever expanding possibilities.

As I mentioned earlier, if you find yourself eating more than a few servings a day, it most likely means you still have emotional and/or physical cravings that need to be addressed. Refer back to Chapters 1-3 for more guidance and support. Also, if you are suffering from severe digestive disorders, like Leaky Gut, clear the recipes with your health care practitioner before diving in.

Ingredients to Stock in Your Pantry That Will Help You Create Nutritious Treats

*Please note: If you cannot find the listed items locally, some good resources are Amazon.com and MountainRoseHerbs.com.

~ Items that need to be prepared ~

Raw Almonds, Soaked and Dehydrated

Pour enough water to cover your almonds generously (I usually soak at least 2 Cups at a time). Soak for at least 12 hours. Then, be sure to rinse well before dehydrating overnight (12-16 hours) at 105 degrees. You can use these nuts as snacks, or you can make your own almond flour with a food processor. I sometimes make my own almond flour, because commercial nut flours do not use soaked nuts, making them much harder to digest. I also toss them in other cookie recipes or in my Crazy-Good Crumble Crunch.

Raw Buckwheat Groats, Soaked and Dehydrated

Buckwheat is often thought of as a grain, yet it is actually a seed. It has no relation to wheat and therefore, is gluten-free. After it has been soaked and dehydrated, it is like a super nutritious "rice crispy", as it adds a wonderful crunchiness to your raw snacks and treats.

You can soak as much as you like, but I usually do about 2-3 cups at a time.

Pour your raw buckwheat groats into a container, making sure that it has room to double in size, as soaking it will make it expand dramatically. Then pour in twice the volume of water, and let it soak for 8-16 hours in the refrigerator. I usually do it at night or late afternoon, so that it can soak overnight and be ready for rinsing in the morning.

After it is soaked, pour your groats into a mesh colander to rinse. The buckwheat will produce a slimy texture after it is soaked. You will want to wash that "slimy film" off, so be sure to rinse really well. I use my hands to move the buckwheat around the colander and rinse for a couple of minutes. Then, spread your rinsed buckwheat out on your Paraflex sheet on your dehydrator tray and dehydrate overnight (approx. 24 hours) at 105 degrees. When it is done it will be light and crunchy. Store in a cool dry place in an airtight container. It will keep for several months.

Raw Walnuts, Soaked And Dehydrated

Most nuts and seeds need to be soaked in order to make them easy to digest. Soak your walnuts in a bowl or container of water for at least 6 hours (I do at least 2 Cups at a time). I like to do it overnight. Then, in the morning, just rinse and spread out on to your dehydrator tray for 12-16 hours at 105 degrees.

~ Healthy Fats ~

Extra Virgin Cold Pressed Coconut Oil

Entire books have been written on all the ways coconut oil can be used for healing, both internally and externally. It has been shown to increase brain function, reduce LDL and increase HDL, kill harmful bacteria and viruses, it is even great to massage into your skin and scalp for deep moisturizing. And, it is ok to use at high heats for cooking. This oil is an integral part of your new frontier of food! I encourage you to do your own research on all its wonderful uses as much has been written about its extensive healing properties.

Grass-Fed Ghee

For those of you that love the taste of butter, but cannot tolerate the effects of dairy, ghee is your new best friend. It is also known as "clarified butter". It not only adds wonderful rich flavor to your desserts, it is stable at high heats, and it is rich in vitamins A, D, and E.

~ Spices and Flavors: ~

Celtic Sea Salt

Celtic Sea Salt contains rich, unprocessed minerals unlike the white table salt that we have become so accustomed to. Lack of minerals in our diet is a major contributing factor to a whole host of health problems, including osteoporosis, thyroid dysfunction, and fatigue. Himalayan salt is also a great alternative, yet the mineral content in Celtic is higher.

Cinnamon Powder

This is one of my favorite super spices as it has numerous health and healing benefits. Some of the biggest benefits include balancing blood sugar, killing Candida, boosting energy, supporting weight loss and improving skin health. I use organic, rich flavored cinnamon for many of my recipes, or I simply sprinkle it in my tea or chocolate smoothies. Works great with chocolate, coffee, and vanilla flavors. Note: the Ceylon variety is better than the Cassia.

Dandy Blend

This is a wonderful caffeine-free, coffee substitute made from chicory and roasted dandelion. Great to use in chocolate recipes to give it a mocha flavor, or as a warm beverage sweetened with a touch of stevia. For an added treat, plop a spoonful of *So Delicious Sugar-Free Coconut Ice Cream* on top of a warm brew for a super soothing evening dessert.

Essential Oils

Lemon, Lime, Peppermint, and Grapefruit are the first ones I recommend for your Sweet Treat Pantry. The main criteria you follow when selecting your essential oils is that your oil be labeled CPTG (Certified Pure Therapeutic Grade) or COTG (Certified Organic Therapeutic Grade). I primarily use *doTerra* Oils in my kitchen, as I appreciate the high quality and deep flavors. To learn more about *doTerra* you can visit my site at: http://SweetHealing.com

Organic Vanilla Bean Powder

This is a wonderful ingredient to use in all of your tasty treats, as it adds such a depth of flavor unmatched to the alcohol filled vanilla extract we are accustomed to. It costs a bit more, but it's worth it and so are you!

~ Super Foods ~

Organic Raw Cacao Powder

This is unprocessed sugar-free, raw chocolate powder. It is divinely rich in anti-oxidants and acts as the base for all of your chocolate delights.

Chocolate opens the capillaries in your brain, so it is great to add super foods to your cacao concoctions for greater absorption of minerals and nutrients.

Goji Joy

Goji Joy is a bliss-inducing and immunity-boosting goji berry extract powder with 10 times the power of whole goji berries! It has a candy-like sweetness but contains almost no fructose. Whole dried goji berries are about 50% fructose, while Goji Joy is about 5% fructose. Goji also has 9 essential amino acids. Fantastic added to berry smoothies or chocolate to increase anti-oxidant and protein content. To learn more about this fabulous super food, visit my site: http://SweetHealing.com

Hibiscus Flower Powder

A wonderful tart flavor to add to your berry blends. It has very high levels of anti-oxidants and vitamin C. Its wonderful pink color also adds a lovely pink tint to your desserts. It can be found on http://MountainRoseHerbs.com.

Longevity in a Bottle

This is the most comprehensive mix of food-medicine I've found on the market today. It brings together 40 of the most revitalizing, anti-aging, deeply energizing super foods and herbal extracts all into one bottle. It is wonderful to pair with chocolate, vanilla or coffee flavors. To learn more visit my site: http://SweetHealing.com

Maca Bliss

Maca Bliss is extracted from 10 pounds of whole dry maca. It's a wonderful super food that can help increase energy, build resilience to stress, balance hormones, and increase libido. I like this particular brand because of its malty taste and careful extraction process. It has a wonderfully sweet, caramel-like flavor that works great with coffee and chocolate. To learn more, visit my site: http://SweetHealing.com

Maqui Powder

The purple Chilean maqui berry is one of the most antioxidant-rich foods. It has a wonderfully tart flavor that pairs well with berries, chocolate and vanilla. It also contains an abundance of vitamin C, calcium, iron, potassium, anti-aging anthocyanins and polyphenols, and anti-inflammatory compounds.

Mesquite Powder

Also known as mesquite flour or mesquite meal. It has a malt-like flavor with a hint of caramel. High in protein and soluble fiber, it is an excellent (partial) flour replacement in baked goods. Tastes great in teas, coffees, chocolate, and smoothies.

Mushroom Immunity

Mushrooms have been used in every human culture for 1000's of years to promote strong health and longevity. This mix has the widest array of all these potent mushrooms in one bottle. Each species contains a unique array of polysaccharides (essential sugars) and novel compounds that strengthen the immune system. The flavor pairs wonderfully well with coffee and chocolate. To learn more, visit my site: http://SweetHealing.com

~ Sweeteners ~

Coconut Palm Sugar

Low on the glycemic index and adds wonderful minerals to your snacks. It is particularly high in magnesium, potassium, iron and zinc, and is a natural source of the vitamins B1, B2, B3, B6 and C. I use sparingly as a sugar substitute.

Lucuma

This low-glycemic dried fruit powder contains many nutrients including beta-carotene, iron, zinc, vitamin B3, calcium and protein. It has a unique, caramel-like taste that pairs great with ginger, vanilla and raw honey.

100% Real Maple Syrup

A wonderful sweetener to add a rich brown sugar flavor to your treats. It's packed with anti-oxidants and anti-inflammatory compounds. Great to pair with stevia as it adds a wonderful balance of sweet flavor.

Raw Organic Honey

Raw honey is loaded with immune boosting agents (particularly Manuka Raw Honey. It has been shown to heal MRSA!). This wonderful sweetener is also great for populating the good bacteria. Raw Honey is NOT the same as regular honey you find at a typical grocery store. Unless it is labeled "raw", the quality of honey has been destroyed in the manufacturing process and might even have high fructose corn syrup added. It's best to buy Raw Local Organic Honey, to help your immune system fight off the local pollens and allergens.

Stevia, Powdered and Liquid

I like to use powdered KAL Brand Powdered Stevia in most of my recipes. It is very purely processed and it is much sweeter than other brands I have tried, so a tiny bit goes a long way. When sweetening tea or smoothies, the Omica Liquid Brand is also great. You also might like flavored liquid versions, such as vanilla or toffee, as they can add a wonderful hint of deliciousness to your drinks and desserts.

Yacon Syrup

A dark, slightly sour, sweetener similar to molasses yet is very low on the glycemic index. Good for feeding the healthy bacteria and considered "ok" for diabetics to use as an alternative sweetener. Works well with chocolate, coffees, and teas.

~ Miscellaneous Must Have's ~

Bob's Red Mill Gluten Free Flour

This flour is not only gluten-free, but grain-free. It is made entirely of ground beans. Works great as a supplemental flour for a more cakey-like texture in baked goods. Can be found at most health food stores, Costco or Amazon.com.

Arrowroot Powder

Can be used as a gluten-free binder instead of wheat flour. Great for baking, pancakes, or thickening sauces.

Chia Seeds

Chia is one of my favorite seeds because it is so dense in healing nutrients: protein, omega-3's, vitamins, minerals and fiber (6 grams in 2 T.) So, say goodbye to your damaging laxatives with this wonderful gift from Mother Nature. Chia will do the trick! Because it is so rich in fiber, it does wonders to help balance blood sugar and reduce cholesterol. It also has a variety of textures depending on how you use it. When chia seed is soaked in a bit of water, it makes a wonderful thickening agent that can be used in place of eggs (1 T. ground chia soaked for 5 mins in ¼ C. water to replace 1 egg), or as a pudding-like cereal for breakfast. Or, if left dry, it adds a wonderful crunch to your diet. I use it inside my dessert recipes and as a topping to homemade healthy ice creams and smoothies.

Hemp Seeds

These fabulous seeds are one of nature's perfect foods. Hemp seed is rich in protein, omega-3 fatty acids, vitamins and enzymes. It has no starch or sugar, and it helps to reduce inflammation, cholesterol, and high blood pressure. It's soft nutty texture makes it a nutty addition to salads, smoothies and homemade ice creams. When blended, it creates a wonderful creamy texture and great alternative to protein powders.

~ For Culturing Foods ~

Kefir Starter

Used to make your coconut kefir water. I recommend the Kefir Starter from BodyEcology. You can find the link to this site on http://SweetHealing.com

Vegetable Culture Starter

Used to make your cultured vegetables. I recommend the Vegetable Culture Starter from Caldwells or Culture Starter from Body Ecology. You can find the link to Body Ecology on http://SweetHealing.com and the link for Caldwell's at http://CulturedFoodLife.com

Eco Bloom from Body Ecology

EcoBloom is pure chicory root that is a prebiotic (food for good bacteria). It is used in making your cultured foods or it can be added to smoothies to feed your inner bacterial garden. To purchase, visit http://SweetHealing.com and click on the Body Ecology link.

Ancient Minerals from Body Ecology

High quality minerals to add to your cultured vegetables, making them even more nutrient rich. Link to Body Ecology can be found on http://SweetHealing.com

Okay, now that you have become acquainted with your beautiful ingredients, you are ready to make some nourishing treats!

RECIPES: Crafting Divine Desserts

The recipes I have included in this book are ones that I use on a regular basis. I have designed them to be low in sugars, gluten-free, grain-free, dairy-free, nutritious, delicious, and super easy to make. I've made an effort to offer a wide variety of sweet sensations to satisfy various moods. They are meant to give you a taste of what is possible. My hope is that you will be inspired to add your own personal flavor twists, letting yourself get creative, and expanding your repertoire of sweet sensations.

If you have any questions or comments about any of the recipes, feel free to contact me via my website at: http://SweetHealing.com

Recipe Legend:

T. = Tablespoon
tsp. = Teaspoon
C. = Cup (8 ounces)

Mixed Berry Compote

Many of my recipes will include the bountiful berry because berries are not only loaded with fiber, which helps you feel full (and eat less), but they top the charts in anti-oxidant power, protecting your body against inflammation and free radicals (molecules that can damage cells and organs). One study even showed that one-half to one cup of mixed berries a day improved cognition and motor performance. So, be sure to eat a wide variety of this fabulous, wholesome treat!

This recipe is a wonderful sweet and tart sauce that is great to keep in the refrigerator as a healthy indulgence for all sorts of things. I like to put it on my protein pancakes or drizzle it on my *So Delicious Sugar Free Vanilla Coconut Ice Cream*. It's even great at Thanksgiving as a cranberry sauce alternative.

After it is jarred, it can be easily stored in the pantry, or you can pack it up into small containers and freeze it for future use.

Ingredients:

1 bag of Organic Mixed Berries (I use a 3 lbs frozen bag from Costco)
⅓ C. Xylitol or Coconut Palm Sugar
¼ C. Lemon Juice
2 Organic Apples, cored and peeled
⅛ tsp. KAL Stevia Powder
2 Pinches of Celtic Sea Salt
¼ tsp. Vit C. Powder

1. Pour bag of berries into large pot. Turn heat to med high.
2. Pick out most of the large strawberries, and blend with apples in high-speed blender.
3. Pour apple mixture into the large pot with the rest of the berries.
4. Heat up to med-high and stir. If the berries are frozen it will take a bit more time for the berries to soften and blend.
5. Press the berries against the side of the pot with a big spoon until the berries are well mashed.
6. Add the rest of the ingredients and bring to a boil, stirring and pressing for 10-15 minutes. Be sure to let the mixture boil for at least 10 minutes. When you reach the desired consistency, you are done.

You can store in small containers to freeze and pull them out when you want some compote for the week. Or, jar into sterilized jars and store in the pantry for months.

I like to jar my compote as they make wonderful gifts and last for at least a year. The small 4-ounce or 8 ounce Bell Jars work wonderfully.

To Jar:

1. In a large soup pot, boil your jars and lids for 15 minutes.
2. Pull them from the hot water with jar tongs.
3. Pour compote into each jar leaving ¼ inch at the top to allow the hot mixture to expand.
4. Secure lid and let cool. Should make 6-12 jars, depending on jar size you choose. Store in a cool, dry place.

Protein Pancakes

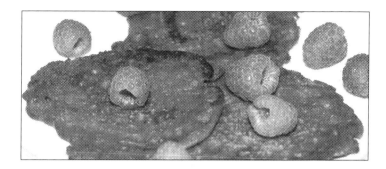

This recipe is a wonderful way to get your pancake fix without zapping your energy out for the rest of the day. The protein helps to balance your blood sugar, and using my berry compote instead of copious amounts of maple syrup will send you into the more heavenly hemispheres of human existence.

Ingredients:

⅓ C. Bob Red Mills Gluten Free Flour
4 T. Vanilla Protein Powder (Rice or Whey)
2 T. Arrowroot Powder
½ tsp. Aluminum Free Baking Powder
¼ tsp. Baking Soda
1/16 tsp. (just a pinch) KAL Brand Stevia Powder
½ tsp. Cinnamon
⅛ tsp. Celtic Sea Salt
2 tsp. Vanilla Extract
¼ tsp. Vanilla Bean Powder, optional
¾ C. Water

1. Mix dry ingredients.
2. Add Vanilla to water, then whisk liquid into dry mix.
3. Whisk until smooth.
4. Pour spoonfuls into hot pan, greased with coconut oil. Pancakes work best if they are no more than 3-4 inches in diameter. The

batter will not be thick like American pancakes, but rather thin like a Swedish pancake. And, because they are thin, they will cook faster than regular pancakes.

5. Flip when bubbles start to form, about 30 seconds to 1 minute. After they are flipped over, they should be done in 15 to 30 seconds.

6. Top with a bit of Ghee or Coconut Oil and Berry Compote. Yum.

Makes 10-12, 4-inch pancakes. Store batter or pancakes in refrigerator.

Tart Apple Berry Crumble Pie

This is a wonderful tart and fruity dessert that will satisfy that cry for pie, without the gluten or any grains. I like to serve it with *So Delicious Sugar Free Vanilla Ice Cream* and my Mixed Berry Compote.

Ingredients:

5 Med. Organic Apples, sliced ⅛ inch thin
¼ tsp. Cinnamon
2 T. Lemon Juice
¹⁄₁₆ tsp. KAL Brand Stevia Powder
1 T. Arrowroot Powder
2 tsp. Xylitol or Coconut Palm Sugar
Pinch of Celtic Sea Salt
½ C. Berry Compote, optional (recipe above)
1 tsp. Ghee, to grease the pie dish

1. Chop your apples slices into small chunks. Then, mix all ingredients, except for the berry compote in large bowl.
2. Spread mixture evenly into ghee greased 10-inch pie pan, small 4 inch pie tins pan for individual pies.
3. Pour the Berry Compote over the top of the apple mixture, then set aside and mix together the Crumble Topping below.

Crumble Topping

Mix:

¾ C. Almond Flour
½ C. Bob's Red Mill Gluten Free Flour
½ tsp. Celtic Sea Salt
¼ tsp. Cinnamon
½ tsp. Vanilla Bean Powder
¹⁄₁₆ tsp. KAL Brand Stevia Powder
1 T. Lucuma Powder
2 tsp. Coconut Palm Sugar
⅓ C. Chopped Walnuts

Combine, then add:

¼ C. Coconut Oil, melted
1 T. Ghee, melted, optional
½ tsp. Vanilla Extract

1. Mix all dry ingredients, then add vanilla extract to melted coconut oil and ghee, then add to dry mix. Mix with hands until crumble forms.
2. Sprinkle on top of Apple/Berry Mixture.
3. Bake at 350 degrees for 35-40 minutes for large pie or 20-30 mins for small pies.
4. Then, place aluminum foil over the pie (to avoid burning the crumble topping), and bake 5 more minutes or until apples are soft and mixture is bubbling.
5. Cool and Serve with *So Delicious Sugar Free Vanilla Coconut Ice Cream* and more Berry Compote. Mmmmm.

Crazy-Good Crumble Crunch

This little treat is one you'll enjoy for many occasions. I enjoy it as a little snack in the morning with my tea, but it's really good anytime. It also travels well and is a great little pick-me-up treat in the afternoon. You can eat it as is, or crumble it over *So Delicious Sugar Free Coconut Ice cream*. See the Berry Compote recipe for making your own little sundae.

Mix together:

2 T. Raw Honey
1 T. Water
2 T. Raw Almond Butter (or any raw nut butter of your choice)
½ tsp. Cinnamon
½ tsp. Vanilla Bean Powder
⅛ tsp. Clove Powder
½ tsp. Anise Seed
Dash of nutmeg
Pinch of Cayenne Pepper
½ tsp. Celtic Sea Salt (sprinkle a touch more at the very end)
4 drops Liquid Stevia

Add to mixture:

1 C. Walnut pieces, soaked and dehydrated
½ C. Almonds, soaked and dehydrated
½ C. Pecans, soaked and dehydrated, optional
1 C. Hemp Seeds

½ C. Sunflower Seeds, soaked and dehydrated
1 ¼ C. Raw Buckwheat, soaked and dehydrated (see process in pantry list)

1. Mix together honey, nut butter, all the spices, and stevia in a large bowl.
2. Add your nuts and seeds. Feel free to change up the recipe, adding the specific seeds and nuts that you prefer.
3. Mix well, until a clumpy mix forms.
4. Spread your mix onto your Paraflex sheet that lies on your plastic dehydrator tray. Press it down firmly so that it makes a large, compact cookie.
5. Dry in your dehydrator for 26-28 hours (until crunchy) at 105 degrees. Break apart and place in an airtight container.
6. Store in an airtight container in a cool, dry place (do not refrigerate). Makes about 6 cups of Crumble Crunch.

Enjoy as a breakfast or afternoon snack. Travels well too!

Bonus Breakfast Porridge Recipe:

This is another great way to use your Crumble Crunch in the morning. This little porridge will set you up for the day, giving you a boost of fantastic fiber and Omega 3's to keep everything on the move.

Soak 1 ½ T. Chia Seed in ½ C. Unsweetened Almond Milk for 5-10 mins (until thick, like a runny porridge. Add more chia if you like it thicker.)

Add:

1 tsp. Raw Honey
Pinch of Vanilla Bean Powder
Top with 2 tsp. Berry Compote, optional
Sprinkle Crumble Crunch on top

Enjoy!

Gluten-Free Vanilla Berry Cake

This recipe makes a fabulous alternative to sugar-crusted coffee cake for that special morning brunch. Or, instead of that afternoon sweet splurge, make a batch of these healthy moist muffins to tie you over for the week. Personally, I like it as a breakfast or afternoon snack with tea.

A little story about kids: I left 2 of these muffins on the counter for my 16 year old son and his friend, Henry. Henry loved them so much he said to my son Alex, " Hey Dude, I'll pay you a dollar for your muffin!"

Made me laugh. So, let this be a testament that kids don't necessarily love junk food. They just like food that tastes good!

To substitute the eggs with Chia Seed:

Yield: 1 egg replacement ~
1 T. Chia Seed, ground
¼ C. Water

Mix the water and ground chia seed meal in a small bowl. Allow to sit for 5 mins, or until it takes on a goopy texture similar to raw egg yolk.

Mix together:

2 C. Almond Flour
⅓ C. Bob's Red Mill Gluten Free Flour

2 ½ tsp. Baking Powder – Aluminum Free
1 tsp. Baking Soda
¼ + ⅛ tsp. KAL Stevia Powder (Adjust if using a different brand)
1 tsp. Vanilla Bean Powder
½ tsp. + ⅛ tsp. Celtic Sea Salt

Whisk, then fold into dry mix:

2 Eggs or Chia Mixture
1 ½ T. Vanilla Extract
2 T. Maple syrup or 2 ½ T. Xylitol with 1 T. Water
¼ C. Water
1 T. Lemon Juice
2 T. Ghee, melted, optional
⅓ C. Mix of Coconut Oil + Ghee or just Coconut oil, melted

Sprinkle on Top of muffins or cake before baking:

½ C. Frozen or Fresh Raspberries or Blueberries

1. Mix all dry ingredients.
2. Whisk wet ingredients, except berries.
3. Carefully fold wet mixture into blended dry mixture. Batter will become slightly puffy due to the baking soda being added to a moist mix. Be careful not to mix too rigorously, as you want to maintain the puffiness of the batter. This will make for a lighter, more "cakey" muffin.
4. Spoon into paper cup lined muffin tin. Fill cups evenly full.
5. Sprinkle berries on top of cupcakes before putting into oven, or gently fold them into the batter.
6. Bake at 350 degrees for 19-25 mins in paper cup lined muffins tins (cake made with eggs will cook faster than those cooked with chia mix). Or, grease an 8 x 8 inch pan and bake for 22-30 mins until lightly firm in the middle.

7. Serve plain, with Mixed Berry Compote, or spread with Coconut Oil, Ghee, or Butterscotch Butter (see recipe on http://www. thelongevityrecipe.com).

Refrigerate or freeze in airtight container to keep fresh. Makes 12 muffins or one 8 x 8 inch cake. When reheating, remove from paper-liners first, otherwise muffins will stick to paper when warmed. Enjoy!

Gluten-Free Cranberry Banana Nut Muffins

This is one of our family favorites. These are great for any holiday or breakfast gathering. They are not only gluten-free, but grain-free. The sugars are only from natural sources, and the delicious sweetness will satisfy even the most discerning dessert palate. I like to spread on a little ghee or coconut oil with my Berry Compote when they are warm from the oven.

To substitute the eggs with Chia Seed:

Yield: 1 egg replacement ~
1 T. Chia Seed, ground
¼ C. Water

Mix the water and ground chia seed meal in a small bowl. Allow to sit for 5 mins, or until it takes on a goopy texture similar to raw egg yolk.

Mix dry ingredients:

2 C. Almond Flour
⅓ C. Bob's Red Mill Gluten Free Flour
2 ½ tsp. Baking Powder - Aluminum Free
1 tsp. Baking Soda
I tsp. Cinnamon
½ tsp. KAL Brand Stevia Powder
1 tsp. Celtic Sea Salt
1 tsp. Vanilla Bean Powder

Whisk wet ingredients in a separate bowl:

1 ½ T. Vanilla Extract
2 Ripe Bananas, mashed with fork
1 T. Maple Syrup or 2 T. Xylitol with 1 T. Water
¼ C. Water
2 Eggs or Chia Mixture

Add after wet mix is folded into dry mix:

½ C. Dried Cranberries

Sprinkle on top:

½ C. Walnuts, soaked and dehydrated

1. Mix all dry ingredients, except walnuts and cranberries.
2. Whisk wet ingredients.
3. Fold wet mix into dry mix. Gently add cranberries.
4. Pour into 8 x 8 Pyrex pan. Or, pour into muffin tins lined with paper cups. Fill cups full. Then, sprinkle walnuts on top.
5. For large cake, bake at 350 degrees for 25-30 mins. For muffins, bake at 350 degrees for 15-19 mins. Done when slightly golden and firm to the touch. Makes 12 muffins or one 8 x 8 cake.

The Raw Chocolate Section

I devoted a small section to chocolate because of its particular healing properties. Unlike processed dark chocolate, anti-oxidants are preserved in raw cacao. Benefits from keeping organic chocolate unheated include: much higher levels of anti-oxidants as well as the preservation of vitamin C, phenethylamine (PEA, the feel good neurotransmitter responsible for the feeling of love!), Omega 6 fatty acids (which when heated become rancid and cause inflammation), tryptophan (a commonly deficient amino acid in those who consume a diet of mostly cooked food), and serotonin.

Cacao is also the highest whole food source of magnesium, which also happens to be the most deficient mineral in our modern diet, especially for women. Some would even argue that it is more important than calcium because without it, calcium cannot be absorbed. Magnesium also relaxes muscles, improves peristalsis in the bowels and relaxes the heart and cardiovascular system. The dark chocolate anti-oxidants have been clinically proven to aide in reversing heart disease and causes naturally lower blood pressure. Also, various other vitamins and minerals in raw cacao benefits the cardiovascular system.

Its uses are really endless, but I have included some of my most favorite, super easy recipes to help you get acquainted with making your own special raw chocolate treats.

After you try these, my hope is that you will no longer lust after the ones you see in the grocery store, as yours will not only taste better, but will give you a boat-load of energizing nutrients and fabulous fats!

Super Simple Chocolate Chunks

This is a recipe that is perfect for the person that loves chocolate, yet wants to get off the sugary stuff or super expensive specialty options at the grocery store. You do not have to be an experienced Chocolatier to make it. In fact, it's hard to mess up. This is a deeply nutritious treat that satisfies the chocolate craving, while delivering a whole host of powerful anti-oxidants and healthy fats.

This chocolate is just a base recipe; you can add endless amounts of ingredients to play with flavor and added health benefits. I highly recommend getting creative with the super foods, herbs, and essential oils listed below. It's so much fun to experiment and add super nourishing ingredients. Plus, you get so much more bang for your bite!

Remember chocolate opens the capillaries in the brain allowing for greater absorption of minerals and nutrients, so it is a great idea to mix in super foods, spices and/or essential oils to this amazing gift from the gods.

Blend in High Speed Blender:

1 C. Coconut Oil, melted
2 T. Ghee, melted (or melted coconut oil)
1 C. + 2 T. Organic Raw Cacao Powder
1 T. Maple Syrup

1 T. Raw Honey

⅛ tsp. KAL Brand Stevia Powder (add more or less, depending on desired sweetness)

¼ tsp. Celtic Sea or Himalayan Salt

1 tsp. Vanilla Bean Powder

½ tsp. Maca Bliss, optional

½ tsp. Mesquite Powder, optional

½ C. Chopped Macadamia Nuts, Pistachios, or Walnuts

¼ C. Dried Pomegranate Seeds or Dried Cranberries, optional

Sprinkle with a dash of coarse Sea Salt on top, optional

8 x 8 Pyrex pan

Parchment Paper to line

1. Pour your melted Coconut Oil and Ghee into your blender. Add the rest of the ingredients, except the nuts, dried pomegranate seeds or cranberries, and coarse sea salt.
2. Blend on medium until creamy.
3. Pour your mixture into a paper lined Pyrex 8 x 8 pan (very easy to remove the chocolate if the pan is paper lined).
4. Let your mixture cool for 10 minutes on the kitchen counter, then sprinkle your nut and dried fruit toppings. I also like to sprinkle a tiny bit of coarse salt.
5. Place the pan in the refrigerator to set up your chocolate completely.
6. When the chocolate is hard to the touch (about 45 mins), remove from pan and cut into ¾ -inch squares.
7. Store your treats in the refrigerator to keep from melting at room temperature. Makes 42-56 servings.

Super Food and Spices to try:

½ tsp. Goji Joy

¼ tsp. Mushroom Immunity

½ tsp. Longevity in a Bottle

¼ tsp. Organic Cinnamon

⅛ tsp. Cayenne

½ tsp. Anise Seed

1 tsp. Maqui Powder

More simple ideas to ponder:

1 -2 drops Peppermint Essential Oil

1 -2 drops Wild Orange Essential Oil

Chocolate Nut-Butter Crunch Bars

These are a real crowd pleaser as they satisfy the sweet tooth and crunch craving. Sometimes I just make the nut butter base without the chocolate topping as a treat all by itself. Both versions make a great snack with tea.

Blend in Food Processor:

¼ C. Raw Almond or Cashew Butter
2 Medjool Dates, pitted
1 C. Walnuts, soaked and dehydrated

Add:

2 tsp. Raw Honey
⅛ tsp. KAL Brand Stevia Powder
½ tsp. Celtic Sea Salt
1 tsp. Vanilla Bean Powder
¼ tsp. Cinnamon
1 tsp. Mesquite Powder
⅓ C. Chia Seed
2 T. Coconut Oil, melted

Pulse gently into mixture:

½ C. Buckwheat, soaked and dehydrated (should be light and crunchy)

1. Blend the first 3 ingredients, and then add the rest of ingredients except for the dehydrated buckwheat. Blend well.
2. Add buckwheat, and pulse through your dough gently, as you don't want it to become emulsified into your mixture. You want to keep that crunch!
3. Press nut butter dough into paper lined 8 x 8 inch Pyrex pan. If you want a little more crunch you can press more buckwheat into the top of your dough along with a sprinkle of added sea salt (adds more flavor).
4. Set aside and refrigerate while you are making the chocolate topping below. Or, if you don't want to add the topping, refrigerate for at least 45 mins, then cut into squares. Enjoy as a nut-butter crunch bar.

Chocolate Topping

½ C. + 1 T. Raw Cacao
½ C. + 1 T. Coconut Oil, melted
1 T. Maple Syrup + 1 T. Raw Honey
⅛ tsp. KAL Brand Stevia Powder
¼ tsp. Vanilla Bean Powder
⅛ tsp. Celtic Sea Salt

1. Blend all ingredients in a blender until smooth.
2. Pour onto your chilled nut butter dough and spread evenly.
3. If you like, you can sprinkle more dehydrated buckwheat and salt on top of chocolate for added crunch and flavor.
4. Cool in refrigerator until chocolate is hardened, at least 40 minutes.
5. Cut into ¾-inch bites and store in refrigerator in an airtight container. Makes 56-64 squares

Feel free to experiment with super foods. Below are some ones I like to try with this recipe.

For more flavor options, add to chocolate or nut butter mix:

1 tsp. Longevity in a Bottle
½ tsp. Mushroom Immunity
1 tsp. Maca Bliss Powder

Heavenly Chocolate Mousse

This is a non-dairy indulgence that your body will love. This is a great dessert to serve guests that you want to impress. It is also an easy one to change up and add different flavors to your liking.

Blend in high-speed blender:

½ C. Raw Cashews, soaked and rinsed

¼ Ripe Avocado

½ C. Coconut Oil, melted

¾ C. + 2 T. Water

½ C. Raw Cacao Powder

¼ tsp. Celtic Sea Salt

¼ tsp. KAL Stevia Powder (if you want it more sweet, add a bit more)

1 tsp. Vanilla Extract

1 tsp. Vanilla Bean Powder

1 T. Maple Syrup

1 ½ T. Raw Honey

3 tsp. Mesquite Powder

1 tsp. Maca Bliss, optional

1. Soak your cashews for 6-8 hours. Then, rinse.
2. Blend all of your ingredients in a high-speed blender until divinely creamy.

3. Taste your mix to get your preferred "sweetness." Add more maple syrup, honey, or a touch more stevia if you would like it sweeter. Just be careful not to add too much.

4. Pour blended mix into little espresso cups or little bowls and chill in the refrigerator. The mousse will set as it cools.

5. Before serving, let bowls sit at room temperature for 20-30 mins to soften, and top with a sprig of mint and chocolate nibs. For a creamy decadent top, whip up some grass-fed whip cream or coconut cream, add some vanilla powder and stevia to sweeten. Then, pop a dollop on your mousse cups! Mmmmm. Makes 6-8 servings.

Tip for leftovers: If you have some leftover mousse you can easily make it into some rich and creamy ice cream. Just scoop it into your high-speed blender, add 4-6 ice cubes, a little water, a few drops of stevia, and blend away! Feel free to add more cacao, vanilla protein powder (*Tera's Whey Bourbon Vanilla Protein Powder*, works great), or super foods to change up the nutrient content too.

More Flavor Ideas:

1 drop Peppermint Essential Oil
1 drop Orange Essential Oil and dash of cinnamon
Top with fresh berries or Berry Compote

Berry Delicious Chocolate Squares

This chocolate treat has mucho health benefits, as it is combined with berries. The combination of both berries and chocolate exponentially increases the anti-oxidant value of each ingredient.

Mix in food processer:

2 Medjool Dates, pitted
1 ¼ C. Cranberries, dried
Pinch of Celtic Sea Salt
1 T. Coconut Oil, melted
¼ tsp. Vitamin C. Powder
1 tsp. Goji Joy Powder, optional

Add to your blended mix, yet gently pulse:

1 ¼ C. Walnuts and/or Macadamia Nuts

Blend separately in blender:

¾ C. Raw Cacao Powder
⅓ C. + 1 T. Coconut Oil, melted
⅓ C. Ghee, melted (or substitute with coconut oil)
¼ tsp. Vanilla Bean Powder
1 T. Maple Syrup
1 T. Raw Honey

⅛ tsp. KAL Brand Stevia

1 tsp. Maca Bliss, optional

1 tsp. Goji Joy, optional

1. After you have blended your first set of ingredients in your food processor, add your nuts and pulse them in gently. You don't want them to disappear entirely, but to remain small nutty bits.
2. Then, take your dried fruit dough and press it into a paper-lined 8 x 8 Pyrex pan. Press it in evenly as it will be the bottom layer of your berry square.
3. If you like the combination of salt and sweet, take a bit of sea salt and lightly sprinkle over top of bottom layer. Gently press salt into dough.
4. Now, blend the chocolate and other above ingredients in your high-speed blender. If you do not have ghee, that's ok, you can use more coconut oil. However, the ghee will give it a wonderful buttery flavor, and it's full of vitamins A, D and E.
5. Pour your chocolate mix over your berry layer, and place in the refrigerator to cool for at least 45 mins. It must be hard to the touch before you can cut into ¾-inch bite size squares.
6. Store in an airtight container in the refrigerator. Makes 56-64 servings.

Hibiscus Berry Butter Candy

In case you are not a big chocolate fan, these will fit your candy fix. They are a wonderful mix of tart and sweet, with chewy, buttery, vanilla flavors tying it all together. Berries, as you may well know are deeply rich in anti-oxidants and nutrients. The fats and chia seeds are great for your brain and heart health. I have also listed below various essential oil ideas for you to experiment with and become your own candy maker in the kitchen. These are fun to make with kids too!

1 C. Dried Cherries and/or Blueberries (or, *Antioxidant Fusion* at Costco is a great mix)
½ C. Cranberries (sweetened with apple juice preferred)
2 tsp . Maqui Powder
2 tsp. Goji Joy
⅛ tsp. KAL Stevia Powder
2 tsp. Raw Honey
¼ tsp. Sea Salt (Celtic or Himalayan)
1 ½ tsp. Hibiscus Flower Powder or ½ tsp. Vit. C Powder
¼ tsp. Vanilla Bean Powder
⅓ C. Chia Seed, dry
1 C. Coconut Oil, melted
1 ½ T. Ghee, melted (or coconut oil, melted)

1. Mix all ingredients in your food processor until blended, yet still chunky.

2. Spoon oily mixture into candy molds, or pour into an 8 x 8 Pyrex paper-lined square dish.

3. Flatten the mixture with a large wooden spoon. Spread chunky mixture evenly into the corners so that it fills out the square shape.

4. Cool for at least 1 hour in the refrigerator. Make sure that it is level when cooling so that your squares are even in size.

5. Cut into ¾-inch bites. Makes 56-64 bites. Keep in airtight container.

Here are some other flavors you can play with:

1 drop Wild Orange Essential Oil
1 drop Grapefruit Essential Oil
1 drop Lemon or Lime Essential Oil

Ginger-Lime Soft Bites

These are tasty, tart bites of spicy goodness. The lime adds a refreshing twist to the earthy ginger flavors. If you prefer the traditional ginger cookie flavors, just leave out the lime oil and lime juice to both the dough and glaze. For a more playful and festive presentation, you can roll the dough out and use cookie cutters, or simply press the dough into your 8 x 8 Pyrex pan. Then dehydrate, glaze, and cut into diamond shapes.

Blend:

½ C. Coconut Flour
½ C. Walnuts, soaked and dehydrated

Add:

1 tsp. Ginger Powder
¼ tsp. Cinnamon
⅛ tsp. Ground Clove
Pinch of Nutmeg
½ tsp. Celtic Sea Salt
½ tsp. Vanilla Bean Powder
⅛ tsp. KAL Brand Stevia Powder
2 T. Lucuma Powder
2 T. Raw Almond or Cashew Butter
6 Dates, pitted
1 ½ T. Lime Juice

1 drop Lime Essential Oil

¼ C. Coconut Oil, melted

1 tsp. Raw Honey

1. Blend coconut flour and nuts in a food processor.
2. Add the rest of the ingredients and blend.
3. **For Bars:** Place dough into a paper lined 8 x 8 Pyrex pan. Press into pan and then place into a dehydrator for at least 12 hours at 110 degrees. (Timing for dehydrating does not need to be as precise as baking, so if it's an hour or 2 longer, no worries.)
4. After dough has dried for the 12 hours, lift large square from Pyrex pan using the parchment paper as a holder, and place it on one of your dehydrator trays, leaving the paper on the dough. Remove Pyrex pan from dehydrator.
5. Let it dehydrate at 105 degrees in dehydrator for one more hour out of the Pyrex pan, yet still sitting in the parchment paper.
6. The cookie is done when moist, yet dry to the touch.

For Cookie Cutters: Place wet (undehydrated) dough between 2 Paraflex sheets and roll to ¼ inch thick. Cut cookies in desired shapes. Remove extra dough around the cut shape, leaving cookie shape on the Paraflex sheet. Place this cookie-filled Paraflex sheet on your dehydrator tray. Use excess dough to roll out on another Paraflex sheet to make more cut cookies. Place this sheet on another dehydrator tray for dehydrating. Dehydrate for 12-16 hours. Then, cool to glaze.

Lime Glaze:

1 T. Coconut Oil, melted

1 T. Ghee, melted

4 drops liquid Stevia

¼ tsp. Raw Honey

1 ½ tsp. Lucuma Powder

½ tsp. Lemon or Lime Juice

2 drops Lime Oil

1. After dough is dry, mix up the glaze in a small saucepan over low heat.
2. Drizzle over the large dried cookie or small cookie shapes.
3. Chill in refrigerator until glaze is hardened.
4. Cut into bite size pieces and refrigerate in an airtight container. These will keep for 4-6 weeks in refrigerator. Make 36-48 cookies.

~ Nourishing Cultured-Essential Oil Recipes ~

Cleanse and Refresh Lemon-Lime Smoothie

This is a wonderful mid morning, nourishing energy blast. The Lemon and Lime Essential Oils are a restorative and revitalizing tonic. Great smoothie to help you cleanse your liver and start your day refreshed. If you don't have all the ingredients, just use what you have or get creative and throw in what you do have. I tend to pack my smoothies with tons of nutrients! You can always add more stevia and/or essential oils to adjust the flavors.

Makes enough for 1-2 servings

½ C. Coconut Kefir Water
1-2 drops Lemon Essential Oil
10-12 drops Liquid Stevia, modify to your sweet taste
1 ½ inches Cucumber chunk
1 Stalk Organic Celery
½ C. Organic Romaine or Spinach Leaves
1 T. *Vitamineral Green Powder, Vitality Greens,* or your favorite green powder
1 T. Favorite Vanilla Protein Powder
¼ inch slice fresh Ginger, peeled
⅛ of an Avocado
⅛ tsp. Vit. C Powder
½ Organic Whole Lime, unpeeled
1 T. Micro Green Sprouts, optional
½ Green Apple, optional
4-6 ice cubes
Add water if you want it less thick

Blend in high-speed blender. Sprinkle with Chia Seed and/or Bee Pollen if you want added Omega's, protein, and B Vitamins.

Super Berry Sorbet

This is a wonderful evening treat or something to enjoy on a hot afternoon. You won't miss ice cream with this wonderfully nourishing, cold concoction.

Makes enough for 2

½ C. Coconut Water Kefir
1-2 drops Grapefruit Essential Oil
1 scoop *Tera's Whey Bourbon Vanilla Protein Powder*, or favorite vanilla protein powder
1 ½ C. Mixed Berries, frozen (Costco has a great organic mix)
½ C. Raw Spinach, optional
8-15 drops Liquid Stevia, modify to your sweet taste
¼ tsp. Vit. C Powder
4 ice cubes
½ tsp. Goji Joy, optional

Blend in your high-speed blender and enjoy! Sprinkle with chia seed for added crunch, Omega 3's and fiber.

~ The Cherry on Top! ~

Chilly Cherry Lime Cosmo

I had to offer you just a taste of what is possible in your new frontier of alcoholic drinks. Not that I recommend drinking alcohol everyday. However, there are ways that you can enjoy its relaxing effects without feeling depleted afterwards. Below is an easy mix that you can switch up with various fruits. I like cherries because studies have shown that they can reduce inflammation in the body. Makes 2 servings.

1 C. Frozen Organic Cherries (Costco)

⅛ tsp. KAL Brand Stevia

⅔ C. Vodka

1 tsp. Maple Syrup or 1-2 tsp. Xylitol (sweeten to taste)

¼ tsp. Vit. C Powder

¼ C. Coconut Kefir Water

1 drop Lemon Essential Oil

1 tsp. Goji Joy, optional

4 ice cubes, optional

1 Organic Lime, (squeeze ½ Lime Juice on top of each drink)

1. Blend all ingredients except for lime in high-speed bender.
2. Pour into pretty glasses.
3. Squeeze ½ lime on top of each drink.

Cheers!

You Are Self-Nurturing: Championing When You Need It

It was thirty years ago when I first read about the debilitating and toxic effects that sugar has on our bodies. I was stunned to learn how much damage it caused to our organs and mucked up the extraordinary, complicated processes that these organs performed on a daily basis. Yet, sugar was in practically everything. It had become the proverbial *elephant in the room* that few were addressing. As a result, there weren't many tasty sugar-free food options available then so it was easy to simply go into denial. You are beyond denial now.

Simple answers, just like simple sugars, don't work for our bodies and minds. Just as we need complex carbohydrates to digest slowly into the blood stream so as not to blast our system with insulin, we also need to slowly assimilate the reasons why we crave sugar, and we need to find *real* solutions to our nutritional needs while thoroughly enjoying our food, particularly dessert. You have courageously stepped into this new frontier and have already begun to creatively find real solutions for your long-term health and happiness.

Beyond our chemical cravings for sweets, we need to understand what we are *really* yearning for emotionally, and learn to nurture ourselves more richly, sensuously, and honestly. The fact is, most of us have replaced a sense of nurturing with sugary treats since we were kids, and in so doing have caused chemical imbalances in our brains and in our hearts. It's time to listen more deeply, and respond more consciously and more compassionately. I know that you are capable of offering yourself this love and compassion.

Remember, this new frontier isn't about removing all sweets from our lives, we were meant to enjoy sweet flavors! However, what's even more important than eating sweets is discovering and embracing what makes our lives sweet. You deserve a sweet life.

And remember too: you do not need to control your body through compulsive dieting and exercise. You can feel at peace. Simple sugar can lose its seduction and you can be free to enjoy your life without guilt or deprivation. You no longer have to wage war with your body or your esteem. You have a nurturing Future Self. She loves you dearly. Listen for her guidance. Begin with just one new choice and see what develops from there. You are capable of making choices that serve you well.

I'm not at all a purest, and neither must you be. Sometimes I eat sugar and gluten-filled treats. This is rare, not because I'm restraining myself but because I like MY treats better! (Another reason I shared these recipes with you – I hope you'll like YOURS better too!)

What's also become true for me, and I hope you will discover some truth in it for you: that you enjoy feeling good and feeding your body well; that you choose to value your life and your future; and that as the "urge to splurge" on junk diminishes, your life blossoms with truly delicious enjoyment.

You can have a level of healing and understanding that perhaps you never thought was possible. It doesn't have to take you as long as it took me. Step by step, choice-by-choice, you can dream…and live *your* luscious, sweet, nurturing life.

About the Author

After years of art, design, crafting, cooking, dieting, experimenting, meditating, and self-reflection, Ame became a Certified Holistic Health Coach. She received her coach training from the Institute for Integrative Nutrition, where she was educated in more than one hundred dietary theories and practices. She has crafted The Longevity Recipe as a place where she offers free recipes and guidance to help others design a personal whole-food based diet and self-nurturing lifestyle that supports greater vitality and lasting, radiant health. She helps people create a personalized "longevity recipe" that suits their unique body, lifestyle, preferences, and goals. Ame lives with her husband, Philippe and little dog Emma in Novato, California.